If there is a longing in your heart for true rest, for a peace that surpasses understanding, and for the joy of knowing that the love of heaven is for you, then you have come upon the right book. The messages here in these pages reflect the power and pleasure of God poured out upon us through the blood of His precious Son.

MICHAEL HUNTWORK
PRAYER MISSIONARY, INTERNATIONAL HOUSE OF PRAYER (IHOP)
KANSAS CITY

Much gratitude to Timothy Holt for laboring to pull out these deep treasures and truths from Roland Buck's visitations. Ultimately they come from heaven's treasure box and are much-needed revelation for the body of Christ. Devour this book...I did.

SHARNAEL WOLVERTON
TV HOST, "SWIFTFIRE WITH SHARNAEL WOLVERTON"
AUTHOR, KEYS TO THIRD HEAVEN...USING THIRD HEAVEN
REVELATION TO IMPACT A WORLD AND THE SEERS HANDBOOK
FOUNDER, SWIFTFIRE MINISTRIES INTERNATIONAL

Roland gives a gift in his revelation of the blood of Jesus. This book takes such a simple and basic topic from the Bible and demonstrates why it is the most powerful force that not only saves and washes away sin but helps you live your everyday life in deeper relationship with the King. Whether you are seeking peace, joy, hope, love, inheritance, a new mind-set, or just a Savior, *When Angels Speak—Roland Buck on the Power of the Blood of Jesus* opens the door to true freedom and relationship with God.

GABRIEL AHN
YOUNG ADULT PASTOR
HARVEST ROCK CHURCH PASADENA, CA

When Angels Speak—Roland Buck on the Power of the Blood of Jesus is filled with fresh insight into the redemptive work of Christ. It causes us to stop and once again consider this powerful sacrifice that brings us close to the Father. May we all take the time to pause and consider once again what Christ has done for this. This is definitely more than just recommended reading. It is a pathway to intimacy with Him. Thanks again to Tim and his uncle Roland Buck.

REV. DAVID HAUSER
STATE DIRECTOR, CALIFORNIA HEALING ROOMS

The man that entertained angels, Roland Buck, brings us insights about the outstanding power in the blood of Jesus. I am excited about this book's arrival to the body of Christ; it will help every reader to enjoy the benefits of the blood of Jesus.

ROBERTS LIARDON
EVANGELIST
AUTHOR, *GOD'S GENERALS* AND *THE AZUSA STREET REVIVAL*

Pastor Roland Buck of Boise, Idaho, had a vital and oftentimes misunderstood ministry the last years of his life. In my view, the revelations this man of God received are pivotal for this generation to move forward into the end of the age harvest and the fullness of the stature of Christ. The Lord uniquely emphasized the ministry of this pastor to me beginning in 1992. It was through a unique revelatory encounter that I discovered *Angels on Assignment*, which the Lord used to verify clear biblical insights that He was relating to me at that time. From that day until the present time, I have done all that I can in my ministry to see to it that these messages are not lost but recaptured and embraced by this generation of hungry believers. Timothy Holt has done a tremendous job of capturing a portion of this important series of revelations and reiterating them through the book that you hold in your hand. The power of the blood of the Lord Jesus Christ will be more thoroughly understood and appropriated during this generation than any prior. It is through the fullness of the power of the blood that the end of the age bride will come forth in the Lord's nature and ability to reap the greatest harvest of souls in history. More importantly, it will be a harvest of "sons of the kingdom" that clearly exemplify the nature and ability demonstrated in the life and ministry of the Lord Jesus himself, fulfilling the great promise to do the works He did and even greater.

PAUL KEITH DAVIS
FOUNDER, WHITEDOVE MINISTRIES

The subject of the blood of Jesus has birthed a lot of books and a lot of sermons. It is noteworthy when someone comes along with fresh revelation on this very important subject. Such is the case with Roland Buck's messages. You will find perspectives here you might not have known before. Our thanks to Tim Holt for providing these insights for the Body of Christ today!

PASTOR DAVID FISCHER
AUTHOR, *EXPERIENCING GOD'S POWER IN WORSHIP*
LIVING WATERS CHURCH, PASADENA, CA

This book will draw you deeper into the heart of God and the power of His blood!

CHERYL ALLEN
DIRECTOR OF PASADENA
INTERNATIONAL HOUSE OF PRAYER (PIHOP)

WHEN ANGELS SPEAK

ROLAND BUCK
ON THE POWER OF THE BLOOD OF JESUS

WHEN ANGELS SPEAK

ROLAND BUCK
ON THE POWER OF THE BLOOD OF JESUS

ROLAND BUCK
COMPILED BY TIMOTHY HOLT

Oviedo, Florida

When Angels Speak—Roland Buck on the Power of the Blood of Jesus
By Roland Buck
Compiled by Timothy Holt

Published by HigherLife Development Services, Inc.
400 Fontana Circle
Building 1—Suite 105
Oviedo, FL 32765
407-563-4806
www.ahigherlife.com

ISBN: 978-1-935245-06-3

Cover Design: Tracy Jetté

11 12 13 14 - 9 8 7 6 5 4 3

Printed in the United States of America

DEDICATION

I WANT TO DEDICATE this book to Roland Buck. His life and messages have inspired millions and his work will continue to carry on and minister and build up the body until the Lord calls us to His side. While I was in Boise I read what was on his tombstone. It says, "He inspired the faith of others." I thank God for preparing and using my great uncle in getting these messages on the blood out to the church. The truths in this study have liberated me and have deepened my understanding of the cross, which has benefited me greatly during communion time. When I get attacked, hurt, accused, or feel distant, I spend time taking communion and God speaks to me and heals me as I meditate on these truths over and over again.

TIMOTHY HOLT

TABLE OF CONTENTS

THE HEART OF ROLAND BUCK

People were his calling. He was a man who was always there. He cushioned sorrow, repaired souls, lit the way, sold hope, and dispensed brotherhood. He was strong when there was a need for strength. He was compassionate when there was a need for compassion. He was part spiritual advisor, part teacher, part optimist, part dreamer, part builder. He was on constant call to his community. Night and day, winter and summer, at any hour, he was on duty, ready to serve in time of need. With energy and enthusiasm, he built for tomorrow. With efficiency and experience he handled the one and one thousand details of running a successful organization with protocol and good taste. He handled the hundreds of human relationship problems that fell in his path. He had a sympathetic ear, an understanding soul, a friendly smile, and the knowledge obtained over the years that the real hope of the world depended on love, understanding, and faith in God. He believed in beauty. He believed that all human beings should love each other. He knew that his profession demanded integrity and sacrifice. He was a man who was always there. He was a public servant to all mankind. In time of need he was the most valuable man on Main Street.

INTRODUCTION

Roland Buck was an ordinary man who experienced angelic visitations during his lifetime, 1918 to November of 1979. Roland Buck was my uncle, and I was a baby the year he passed away. While I am thankful for the thousands that came to Christ as my uncle shared his visitations and teachings, I don't want my generation to miss out on the revelation shown to my Uncle Roland. God shared holy truths with Roland Buck—first through the Word of God and then by a series of visitations and visions brought to him within a span of two years during the late 1970s. I would encourage you to read some of his supernatural experiences documented in his book, *Angels on Assignment*, published by Whitaker House.

Angels on Assignment will tell you that Roland's first reaction to these supernatural experiences was to try to get out of delivering to others the messages he was given. He valued his credibility among the churches and felt he was risking his reputation and God's if he shared his unusual encounters with angels. However, God moved on Roland's heart until he changed his mind on the matter, and, before he went on to be with the Lord, he spoke and wrote candidly about the visitations and visions he experienced. That is what brings us to this present book, *When Angels Speak—Roland Buck on the Power of the Blood of Jesus.*

One time the angel Gabriel visited my uncle and told him to write down seven truths that were "God's priorities." Gabriel emphasized that God's very first priority was the precious blood of Jesus.

And so, with my family's blessing and Whitaker House's permission, I took the time to honor God and my uncle by transcribing the sixty-seven sermons available on audio recordings and bring to you in this volume the message he received on God's first priority, *When Angels Speak—Roland Buck on the Power of the Blood of Jesus.*

Every one of God's highest priorities is related to God's love and care for people. We all need to know that God is not looking for reasons to reject us but to save us—He is not interested in our failures but longs for our friendship. The message of the blood is that God's wrath has been turned away and His heart is warm toward us now.

When Gabriel appeared to Roland in 1979, Gabriel said, "There is more excitement in the courts of heaven than there has ever been since Jesus came the first time." It has been a generation since this angelic visitation, and so I pass the baton to you. Let's run our race with joy in our salvation and in fellowship with our Maker through the power of the blood of Jesus.

I'd like to share with you a couple of poems that I wrote related to the theme and meat of this book:

EVERLASTING ATONEMENT

Jesus is pleading, His blood is still speaking, not guilty it's saying for me. Everlastingly, it's covering and cleansing me, continually, for free. So all may see His life and beauty shining out through You and me.

SOON WE'LL SEE HIS FACE

Soon the Radiance of Heaven will call us to His side saying, "come up higher My precious bride." There past the white shores, the King's beauty is revealed, every desire is fulfilled. Our clothing will be made out of His righteousness, that sweet smelling fragrance that comes from Jesus' blood and sacrifice, as well as every loving thing we've ever done. Our record books will be opened and we will hear from the Righteous Judge, "well done."

TIMOTHY HOLT

Chapter One

HOW IMPORTANT IS THE BLOOD OF JESUS TO YOU?

THE TRUTHS CONTAINED here came not by any type of research but directly from God's heart to me. One Saturday night I had gone to sleep before midnight, and God began speaking to my heart. I thought I was asleep, but it seemed as though I was awake and listening to Him and even conversing with Him.

He spoke to my heart so definitely and asked me, "How important is the blood of Jesus to you?" It seemed like the eyes of God were right in my heart. I have preached on the blood, and it was what I thought to be of normal importance to me, but this question just penetrated right into my heart. I told the Lord that I knew it was important and that I had preached on it occasionally. But that answer didn't really satisfy God.

He asked me, "If the blood is important to you, then let me ask you some questions about it so I can get your feelings on the blood." Of course He knew all the time anyway, but He asked me more questions. "What is the power of the blood? How great is it?"

"Well," I said, "the power of the blood is the greatest. That blood washes away sin, it covers sin." I started saying a few things about the blood.

The Lord said, "Let Me show you a few things of how important the blood is to Me."

He let me see the worth of the blood, and He worded its value in practical ways. He said the worth of the blood would be determined by the value of the life that that blood flows through. The value of a chicken's blood would be of very little value because it flows through the life of a chicken. The blood of a human being is very, very valuable because it represents and has the value of the life of the person that it occupies. If it's the president of the United States, the value of that blood would be considered a tremendous loss when it was spilled. If a little child is in an accident and blood is spilled, this is also a tremendous loss. Our Father in heaven places great value upon the blood. Then God pointed out that the value of the blood of Jesus is determined by whom it flowed through. And then He said that when you think of the value of the blood, when you think of the power of that blood, think of the power and the value of that life—that in Him dwelt all of the fullness of God. You can't go higher than that. That blood becomes the most valuable ingredient in the whole world because of whom it flowed through.

So God emphasized that night, when I spoke of the blood, to remember that the power of that blood represented all of the power of the universe because the whole Godhead was represented in that blood: God the Father, God the Son, and God the Holy Spirit. The fullness dwelt in Him, so the blood of Jesus that flowed represented the authority and the power of all that there is. And when you think of God taking that blood and giving it to us, He's giving us the most valuable thing in the whole universe!

If it is possible for a person to get excited in his sleep, I was excited when God told me how powerful the blood is. I had it visualized that its power was only in the fact that it was something He used to wash away my sins, but I didn't realize how or where it got the ability to wash away my sins and take care of those things. For that entire night God dealt with me, and He took me from Genesis to Revelation, asking me questions, giving me scriptures—two hundred scriptures I had never searched out. And He burned them into my mind. After I woke up, I wrote out all of these two hundred references, and every one of them was just exactly the way God gave them to me.

These experiences the Lord allowed me to have a part in are not just empty dreams or imaginations. Every time God dealt with me, He brought the Word of God to me with great force and supporting power.

During one angelic visitation, an angel spoke to me about three main areas that God wanted to talk to me about:

- God's character—what He is really like
- Our position in God
- To remind God's people to prepare for that great Judgment Day

We must understand that through the blood of Jesus we have unbelievable favor with God, and He sees us with total favor.

I had read through the Bible many times and had never seen this beautiful truth of God stating that He looks at man from a different level than man himself does. God's eye view is on the topside of this covering; man's eye view is on the underside. This has been referred to practically every time God has dealt with me, so I want to bring it out here. God wants us to know our position in Him. As we desire to live for Him, and we WANT Him as our Lord, the blood covering is there! He sees us like Christ because we are accepted in Him, all wrapped up and covered in His love. With our faith in Him, He wants us to know this position. Think about this for yourself. Do you see yourself right now wrapped up and covered in God's great love? Do you realize you are his special child and nothing can separate you from his mighty love? Glory to God! That is our position in Christ!

Chapter Two

THE CRIMSON TRAIL THROUGH THE BIBLE

A s I think about all of the thrilling messages that the Lord has given to me through angels, I realize that all of them point back to one central truth. This has proven to be the very heart of God, the heart of the Bible, the heart of all history. The very core, the very center of God's message to us—THE SACRIFICE OF JESUS!

Many great truths stand out as beacon lights in God's revelation of Himself to man. We see His love, His knowledge, and His power. We see His foreknowledge and His grace. But no truth occupies the place of importance in God's heart as does the sacrificial blood of Jesus. In this study we will follow a crimson trail through the Bible and discover the unique place given the blood from the beginning to the end of God's revelation of Himself to man.

Now we have four different sections here as God revealed them to me:

By faith Abel offered unto God a more excellent sacrifice than Cain, by which he obtained witness that he was righteous, God testifying of his gifts: and by it he being dead yet speaketh (Hebrews 11:4).

Abel offered a sacrifice that God had ordained, a sacrifice of blood. We learned from this lesson that from the very beginning there can be no approach to God, no fellowship with Him—even by faith—and no enjoyment of His favor apart from blood. There are people who like to say that their faith takes the place of blood. The Bible tells us that our faith can take the place of our own righteousness and good works, but faith can never take the place of blood.

Now God has given us His truth and His grace. His grace makes a way for us, but both truth and grace cannot be brought to us except by the blood of Jesus.

Blood is the one ingredient that follows through on God's demands, His conditional promises, and His grace. So we have nothing to offer God in order to earn anything from God. Even His free gifts come to us by the blood of Jesus.

At Mount Ararat, a new beginning started after judgment had fallen in the form of a flood. And that new beginning began with blood. Noah sacrificed to God, and that blood was spilled in order to begin fellowship again. Just like that dispensation when Adam and Eve were banished from the Garden of Eden, fellowship with God happened when God covered this man and his wife with the skin of an animal. It started with blood. In Genesis nine, the first thing that Noah did was sacrifice an animal. The Bible says that Noah took every clean beast and offered it as a burnt offering on the altar, and the Lord said it smelled good. He accepted Noah, the sacrifice was favorable to Him, and God gave a covenant to Noah and to forthcoming generations (including ours) with the sign of the rainbow because of that sacrifice that was given.

Now at Mount Mariah we see that trail of blood again on these mountain peaks of the Old Testament where Isaac's life was spared and a nation was formed. But the Word tells us that this nation's beginning was not without blood.

By faith Moses, when he was born, was hid three months of his parents, because they saw he was a proper child; and they were not afraid of the king's commandment (Hebrews 11:23).

Then when the children of Israel went down into the land of Egypt, another new beginning was about to happen. The children of Israel were going to be evacuated out of the land of Egypt. Three million people were delivered by blood. God spoke to Moses:

And the blood shall be to you for a token upon the houses where ye are: and when I see the blood, I will pass over you, and the plague shall not be upon you to destroy you, when I smite the land of Egypt (Exodus 12:13).

So blood became significant in the beginning of a whole new day. When a person comes to the Lord and new life begins for him or her, it comes because of the blood.

Great fear has come into many people's hearts because of a misunderstanding of communion. Some have even preached messages that if people take communion in the wrong way they will drink the cup of damnation. But Jesus Himself told a bunch of people, many who didn't even know God at all, "You aren't going to have any life in you if you don't eat of Me and drink of Me." And when He spoke of eating and drinking unworthily, He wasn't speaking about eating and drinking unworthily by just partaking of communion. He said, "You are doing it unworthily when you are putting your faith in anything else outside of this blood." So we see that the cup can be taken unworthily when we partake of communion while thinking, *I'm so good now. I've examined myself—I haven't done anything bad here.*

There is a feeling of spiritual achievement that people have had because other people have told them they can make themselves ready to take communion by their own efforts. That has denied God's blessing and God's smile for thousands of people down through the years. I'm so glad and thankful that God let this truth surface that the blood of Jesus Christ is just as available and more needed to the one who doesn't know Jesus than the one who does. So that's the reason why I tell people if we will put our faith in what Jesus has done and take the cup, then by taking that cup of communion we are saying something to God that we haven't been able to say in any other way: "God, I'm putting my faith in what this cup symbolizes—the blood of Jesus. This is Your source of life."

I was partaking in a communion service in my office one day when God burned verses from 2 Chronicles 30 into my mind. God let these people know that He's a lot more concerned about people than He is about procedure. There were many in the congregation who were not sanctified. In fact, the Word of God says that the multitude of people had not cleansed themselves, yet they ate of the Passover.

But Hezekiah prayed for them saying,

> "The good Lord pardon everyone that prepareth his heart to seek God" (2 Chronicles 30:18-19).

And the Lord hearkened to Hezekiah, and He healed the people. And He gave them such a revival, there was tremendous gladness. They even defied the tradition. Instead of seven days of feasting, they said, "We can't stop this revival. We've got to go another week!" They said the gladness increased, the joy increased, because God had hearkened, and He had forgiven the people, even bypassing what looked like His own regulations in doing it. This lets us know that the glory of God that is coming today to the world is full of grace and truth. The truth says, "This is how it is," and reveals to man God's way, and reveals to man God's condition.

But so few of us can actually meet God's way with God's conditions. God says they must have help in other ways, so the glory cloud has another segment in it. That other segment is grace—a free gift that comes. God says, this tells you how a situation is, but My grace shows you the way out. So wherever we see God moving by His Spirit, people are finding God—not on the basis of their works, not on the basis of their goodness, but on the basis that God's grace is sufficient.

The second most important truth to me is the grace of God. Blood is on the top of the list of God's requirements, and then grace. When God's covenant, His agreement, came, He said it would only be effective through blood. God said, "Take the blood and sprinkle the altar," which signified God's connection with His people. Now He said, "Take half of it. Half of the blood is for God's side. Now take the other half and sprinkle the people." And God said this blood is the one thing that mankind and God have in common. They divided it. Half of the blood was to take care of the wrath of God so that His wrath is turned away from us. At the cross this happened. The wrath of God smote Jesus. The wrath of God was turned away from us onto Jesus.

God said, "We have one mutual interest. When you say, 'God, I'm putting my faith in the blood,' you are putting your faith in something that I have confidence in. You then become partners with Me. You become part owners with Me in covenant."

The death of Jesus Christ was not only for man; it was for God. There was wrath in God's heart toward man, and that wrath had to be appeased because God was displeased. So the blood of Jesus Christ turned away the wrath of God on that side. That's why God allowed for this beautiful picture, this beautiful symbol. Sprinkle half of it God's way and half of it man's way so that we will have a common meeting ground.

And so at the cross Jesus reached up into heaven with one hand, and He reached down into the earth with the other. That is the joining link right there—the blood is the joining link between God and man. We see in worship, even the golden throne of God, that the altar and the mercy seat in the holy place had to be sprinkled with blood. Without blood, no one could approach the mercy seat. Underneath the golden lid of the mercy seat there was a box called the Ark of the Covenant. Inside that ark, God said mankind has broken the laws of God and every law God saw, and He said, "Moses, take the broken laws of God and put them in that ark. Put this golden lid over the top of this box so that I can't see the broken laws. Now take the blood of the sacrifice and sprinkle it over the top of the mercy seat so that now when someone comes to me asking for mercy I look down and I cannot see the sins because they're hidden under the blood. And every person who comes to me by the way of the blood has identified with the sacrifice that has already been made."

God said that judgment was already meted out to this person because there's the blood. When we come to God through the blood of Jesus, God cannot see one solitary sin. Jesus Christ is the golden covering. His blood and His sacrifice cover every sin that we ever had or ever will commit. There isn't going to be another sacrifice. The weakness of confession is that if it's based on the completeness of our confession, some might miss things because there might be some sin or grievance we committed against God or man that we've forgotten. As a principle, anything that hides us from fellowship with God, that thing separates us from Him and is therefore sin. We need to come and say, "God, I need You. There's something in between us," and God will wipe out that offensive thing.

But, basically, the person who belongs to Jesus doesn't have to come to God and confess a whole lot of things because there's this strong desire to please Him as we walk with God. Twenty four hours a day that blood keeps on flowing. This is the life of the blood that we are going to have in another lesson. It just keeps on cleansing even if we don't even know about it.

We don't have to keep coming to God saying, "God I did this thing, will you forgive me?" God sees the needs of human life, and there would be nothing more insecure in the whole world than salvation if every time something attached itself to us we had to find out about it and run to God for help. We'd be so insecure, nine hours out of every ten we'd be out of fellowship. We'd be lost nine hours out of ten. But when we put ourselves in God's hands and walk with Him, God says when we walk in the light as He is in the light, the blood of Jesus Christ, God's son, is there and we have fellowship with one another. God and us together, we walk through our days, and the blood of Jesus cleanses us from all sin. Some people say that when you're walking in the light you don't have any sin. If this is true, then why did He say that He cleanses us from sin if there wouldn't be any sin there? And if He's cleansed us as we walk with Him, why would we need a further cleansing from sin if when we're walking in the light there's no chance for sin?

What He's telling us is that we're going to have things attach themselves to us, but there's a constant cleansing. There is no life without the blood. When John saw Him, John recognized Him and said, "This is the Lamb of God" (John 1:29). There is no covenant without the blood, but the new covenant begins with blood. Jesus said, "This is my blood of that new covenant" (1 Corinthians 11:25). God's new agreement *is,* "Your sins and iniquities I will remember no more—forever" (Hebrews 10:17). Your faith in His blood is the activating principle; that's what turns the switch on. We're not only freed from the guilt of sin in this life but we're freed from the punishment for sin. The blood that was shed for us is now given to us. That death was for all people, but until they avail themselves and take what God is offering them, they're not able to receive it.

It has already been done for them. Every sin of the world has already been atoned for through the blood of Jesus, and as we take the blood, that blood is given to us. Jesus took that cup, and He gave it to them. And every time we have communion, Jesus is giving us the blood that was shed for us, that life that is greater than all the forces of the universe. The power of the whole Godhead is now taken and given to us. It's a celebration of life because of the power of God, the blood of Christ that is given to us. There's nothing in the whole Bible, and nothing that God does for us that is not tied to the blood of Jesus.

Because of the blood we can suddenly be bold and enter into the throne room. Then comes sanctification and resurrection life. God asked me what the power was that raised Jesus from the dead, and I told Him that it was the power of the Holy Spirit. But He told me that it was the power of the blood. So God let me see three keys. He said, "This blood brings you three keys that will open three barred doors." There's nothing in the whole universe besides the blood that could open these three barred doors:

1. The door of grace
2. The door of heaven
3. The door of God's own heart

When we put our faith in that blood, these three doors are opened to us. We always want to be content with what God has provided for us. When He tells us in scripture, "Be perfect as I am perfect" (Matthew 5:48), He's talking about sharing in His nature and life. He doesn't want us to be the smartest people in the universe but to be people who are like Him in nature. After this earth is gone, the blood will still occupy a tremendous place in God's heart in heaven, and so, from the closing of the gates of Eden to the opening of the gates of heaven, the crimson stream flows. All of the wonders of grace are focused here; His love, righteousness, justification, life, fellowship, joy, and atonement are all but rays of light reflected upon us from the blood of Jesus.

Chapter Three

THE BLESSINGS OF THE BLOOD OF JESUS

I N ALL OF creation we see the intricate detail in God's planning. The
structure of the grass of the field or a leaf on a tree shows evidence of
His thought. From the tiniest insect to His highest creation, we see
the mark of His hand. If we look closely, we can see the intricate detail in
God's planning for the fellowship and oneness we share with Him today.
Think about that. Even the victories over sin and sickness and the divine
life we enjoy in these mortal bodies springs from a divine plan born
in God's heart before the world was made—a plan that is perfect and
complete in every detail. In this plan we see a revelation of God's heart
and His desire and love for man. We see man occupying a bigger place
in the heart and mind of the Creator than any other part of His creation.
In this study we will look at the very heart of redemption by blood and
the blessings it procures:

- Reconciliation
- Cleansing
- Sanctification
- Restoration
- Victory
- Life

Again, I would like to remind you of how detailed God is in all of His creation. Have you noticed even those tiniest insects that look so small are so beautiful, and each of them is put together in such a fascinating way. Each insect has a definite purpose in His overall plan. The world and science call it ecology, but it is actually evidence of God's planning. Each creature fits into His plan. The big fish will eat up the little fish. God knows those big fish will get real hungry, so He has a million times as many fish and eggs that will grow because it is God's plan and God's great cycle.

When we think of the design of God and how it is stamped, I think of the trees by the Kauai river in Hawaii. Did you hear the story about the leaves of those trees? Kauai has more rainfall than any other area around there. God has to make it rain in the area near the Kauai River every day because all the rivers in that area aren't very long and there's not much place to gather moisture. So God just keeps turning on the faucet, piping down all the water needed there. God wanted us to see His handiwork. And so there are literally billions of leaves growing along these rivers, and every one of these trees has a map of this island. It's the shape of the island, and it has the peak in the middle, so the islanders there say that God really smiled on that island and put His mark on all of these trees that line the rivers, each of them showing a design of the island. God did this. And there's hardly anything in nature that you can't find a beautiful design and a reason why He's put it together.

I think of the stag beetle. God made that male beetle with long horns that stick out about four inches. The female doesn't have any horns. But when the butterfly lays her eggs (and they all look alike), she puts the male egg eight inches deeper than the female egg because God told that little old bug that that male beetle had to have some room for its horns to grow after it hatches. Researchers have discovered that there has never been a male beetle egg found less than eight inches from the surface! Talk about design.

Now when God considered the biggest, most important design in His entire universe, don't you think He spent a great deal of time on the big plan? In laying this out He said, "I'm taking my own Son. He's going to be a Lamb who is going to be sacrificed." You were redeemed by the precious blood of Christ in a wonderful plan that was foreordained before the foundation of the world. For the life of the flesh is in the blood. Life is in the blood—this is where the power comes from. So the value of the blood is determined by the kind of life it flows through. This blood that is so precious didn't just flow through an animal or through an ordinary human being. It flowed through one who was given directly from the hand of God. In Him all of the fullness dwells. In Christ's body the fullness of the Godhead dwells.

So we are actually saying that the power of the whole universe is in that blood. Boy, this makes me feel safe! I know that the blood has been applied, and the power of the whole universe is wrapping me up. Life was given to satisfy God's demands. He said without the shedding of blood there can be no remission of sins—we cannot be redeemed without the blood. But when blood covers the individual, sin is so entirely covered and atoned for it can no longer be identified with the transgressor. The worst murderer in the whole wide world can be redeemed. Paul said he was the chief of all sinners, yet when a person puts his faith in that blood, there's an atonement that separates the person from this pile of sin and crime, and there is no way in the entire universe that God has to ever identify that person with his crimes again.

The blood is that great equalizer. People who are way down—it brings them up. And people who are way up—it brings them down. God has it all written out, "Paid in full for everybody." There are a lot of people worried about where their sins are and, through these verses, you can show them where they are—blotted out as a thick cloud and in the depths of the sea. God promises that our sins and iniquities He will remember no more forever.

God has made us His spiritual Israel. The blood destroys the power of sin. The Holy Spirit is His dynamic force. The power of the blood is

God's silent force that works whether you realize it or not. Within you there is a little organ that keeps pumping whether or not you are always conscious that it is beating.

Paul said, "Whether I'm awake or asleep, I am the Lord's." Whether you're sleeping or not, your heart keeps beating.

The same goes for the blood of Jesus. So the blood of Jesus, the great heart of God, just keeps on beating out to you twenty four hours a day, whether you're awake or asleep, or even if you get mad at someone! The blood of Jesus keeps beating out to you as long as your heart's desire is still there to please God. So if our hearts only beat when we thought they were beating, we would be in trouble. So when things go wrong, don't suddenly say, "Heart, start beating!" You don't have to. God says you're tied in with the heart of the universe. It's all right to remind Him, and God won't make fun of you if you do, but He wants us to know that He's on the job all the time.

There's no place in the whole Bible where you could ever read, "Plead the blood." It's not something that displeases God, but it's so comforting when we know that whether we are awake or whether we sleep, the blood keeps on flowing, giving us a constant cleansing! It was the power of the blood that raised up Jesus from the dead. His blood destroyed the power of death, hell, sin, and the devil. His blood gives entrance to eternal life. God's eternal righteousness guarded the most holy place. God said that we can come now because the blood has turned God's wrath away. God's anger is pacified, judgment has been completed. That same Spirit who raised Jesus from the dead will quicken us also through the blood. A lot of people don't realize how intricately God ties His plan all together. The Holy Spirit comes when a person puts his faith in the blood of Jesus.

Chapter Four

THE RECONCILING POWER of
THE BLOOD of JESUS

GOD TOLD MOSES, "Take a vessel of oil and dip your finger into that vessel and put just a little tiny bit on the ear and the thumb and the toe." Those areas indicate the person's thinking, mind, and senses, which point to his or her service and walk. But God says; "Now, Moses, I want to show you the emphasis that I put on the abundance, the joy, the overflowing, and the excitement." So God told Moses to take all the rest of that oil and pour it on the top of his head and let it run down over his beard and down his clothes.

There are a lot of people putting a lot more emphasis on the walk than on the spiritual life. But pouring the largest portion of the oil over the head is God's way of saying that there is more of the Holy Spirit for the abundant life than there is for all of these other things put together. So that's why I jump every once in awhile. If all I did was hard work all the time, it could get kind of boring. But God says you can mix business with pleasure. But this isn't available until the blood of Jesus is applied. So you get the cleansing when you recognize the power of the blood, and when your faith is in that blood it not only makes salvation available to you, it not only opens the door of heaven, but also it makes the power of the Holy Spirit available to you.

> Therefore being justified by faith, we have peace with God through our Lord Jesus Christ: By whom also we have access by faith into this grace wherein we stand, and rejoice in hope of the glory of God. And not only so, but we glory in tribulations also: knowing that tribulation worketh patience; And patience, experience; and experience, hope: And hope maketh not ashamed; because the love of God is shed abroad in our hearts by the Holy Ghost which is given unto us. For when we were yet without strength, in due time Christ died for the ungodly. For scarcely for a righteous man will one die: yet peradventure for a good man some would even dare to die. But God commendeth his love toward us, in that, while we were yet sinners, Christ died for us. Much more then, being now justified by his blood, we shall be saved from wrath through him. For if, when we were enemies, we were reconciled to God by the death of his Son, much more, being reconciled, we shall be saved by his life. And not only so, but we also joy in God through our Lord Jesus Christ, by whom we have now received the atonement. But not as the offence, so also is the free gift. For if through the offence of one many be dead, much more the grace of God, and the gift by grace, which is by one man, Jesus Christ, hath abounded unto many. And not as it was by one that sinned, so is the gift: for the judgment was by one to condemnation, but the free gift is of many offences unto justification. For if by one man's offence death reigned by one; much more they which receive abundance of grace and of the gift of righteousness shall reign in life by one, Jesus Christ. Therefore as by the offence of one judgment came upon all men to condemnation; even so by the righteousness of one the free gift came upon all men unto justification of life. For as by one man's disobedience many were made sinners, so by the obedience of

one shall many be made righteous. Moreover the law entered, that the offence might abound. But where sin abounded, grace did much more abound: That as sin hath reigned unto death, even so might grace reign through righteousness unto eternal life by Jesus Christ our Lord (Romans 5:1-11, 15-21).

As we ponder the power of Jesus' blood, we are reminded once again of the overwhelming love of God. So great was God's love that His entire purpose revolves around His plan to restore man to a place of fellowship. The revelation of His love is seen in all of His dealings with man. It reaches its highest peak in the message of the atonement. This message is woven into every part of the Bible and shows us the importance He places on the completed sacrifice of Jesus.

In this study we will consider the need, the importance, the power, and the results of reconciliation. First of all, let's look at the need.

Sin became a barrier between God and man. There could be no fellowship until this barrier was removed and God's wrath was appeased. A brief picture of this plan is seen in Romans 5:

> Therefore being justified by faith we have peace with God through our Lord Jesus Christ (Romans 5:1).

So we see two of the benefits that have been made available to us through the blood. First of all, we are justified, and secondly, we have peace with God. The separating barrier or wall that sin had raised between us and God is destroyed through reconciliation, and now we have peace with God.

A third benefit made available to us through the blood of Christ is access to God's doorway to grace. The wall between us and God has a doorway, an open access. So He said that through Christ we have access by faith into this grace wherein we stand. We have hope, and we rejoice in hope. In verse five it says, "Hope makes not ashamed because the love of God is shed abroad in our hearts."

Let's bring this message down into the practical realm of our everyday lives. I thought this story was so interesting. I met a pastor's wife in Washington. She was a Native American, and she seemed like she was happy enough to me. But during one of the visitations from Gabriel, he said, "I want you to bring a message to this pastor's wife that she is very special to God. She has a very poor image of herself. She thinks she's worthless. She thinks she's not accepted as she ought to be because of her race. She needs to have this message that God loves her. Tell her that God has put her right where she belongs—that she is special."

Now that's quite a message, so I told her husband. He said, "You can't believe how right-on this message is. She needed to hear that." Then I told them some other things—about this message and why the sacrifice has been so important in the messages that he brought to me. Oftentimes, one of God's angels came to give me a message or show me a picture or vision of a person I would meet in the near future. We just don't know how very much God loves us.

I didn't realize how closely associated Gabriel's function and ministry were to the sacrifice of Christ. I knew from scriptures that Gabriel had given me that he was there, but he built upon this again. He told me the tremendous need that people had of hearing this message that God had taken care of everything and that it was all covered—and then he went into a description of the Old Testament. Let's look at Hebrews 10:11-14:

> And every priest standeth daily ministering and offering oftentimes the same sacrifices, which can never take away sins: But this man, after he had offered one sacrifice for sins for ever, sat down on the right hand of God; From henceforth expecting till his enemies be made his footstool. For by one offering he hath perfected for ever them that are sanctified.

Paul was speaking here, and he said that the sacrifices made at that time for the atonement (before Christ came) had to be made year after year. But in those sacrifices there was a remembrance of sins every year.

Then he told me where I could find these beautiful truths. And he said that men and women who have not recognized the truth of the constant covering that Jesus Christ provided are in the same position exactly as Israel was when they came to the end of the year when the covering was over and it had expired. They were again standing naked and hopeless, helpless before the eyes of the eternal God. All of the charges that were against them were again under review by God. He saw their sins, He saw their guilt.

Then Gabriel told me, "I was present at every sacrifice for the atonement, standing in the presence of God, whose position was above the altar in the holy place. When God moved in, I moved and stood there but unseen."

He also said that the world had forgotten the real meaning of that incense that was to be offered by the priest. He said that while the priest was there and preparing to offer the incense, the whole community was standing and trembling. Their acceptance was based on the observance of certain rules. If the priest would not have thrown in the incense (and you can read this in Leviticus 16:12-13), then he would die because there was no covering. As perfect as he could possibly be made, he still could not do his priestly duties without the covering. So he said the priest was there at the time of the burning of the incense, and as he fulfilled this obligation and the cloud rose and covered him, that God could again smile because the sins were covered for another year. He smelled the sweet savor. The fire of God's wrath struck the incense instead of the priest.

To back this up in scripture—the part about Gabriel standing in God's presence—you can remember that when Zechariah saw this giant angel, it scared him. It scares me, too! But the angel said to him, "Fear not, Zechariah, your prayer has been heard." And farther down it reads, "I am Gabriel that stands in the presence of God. I was sent to speak to you and show you these glad tidings." So you can see through scripture, not just my experiences, that every time Gabriel has appeared with a message, it has been a message of good tidings.

Now I'd like to share with you what he (Gabriel) gave me about Jesus' sacrifice. I wrote this down. He said that as the fire of God's judgment struck His only Son, a cloud ascended that covered all time and all space. It was carried on the wings of grace until it stretched backward across the ages to the beginning of man, erasing all of those charges that kept coming up every year. It spread outward from Calvary across all ages to the end of time, completing a plan that was formed in God's heart before the world began of making man acceptable in His sight.

There's no other way to God except to say, "Jesus, I accept the offering that You made, and I repent. I'm sorry for trying to go my way, and I come back." At that point, the cloud covers you and you're at peace again with God. This is the message that God wants the world to hear today. He wants people to know that the sacrifice is complete and that the cloud is still there.

God wants His people to get this message into their hearts. Get it into your mind—talk about it to people wherever you are. This message of atonement has a three-way message:

1. It has a message to those who are living for God
2. It has a message for those who are careless.
3. It also has a message for the unbeliever to let him or her know the awesomeness of God.

God allowed me to see the Old Testament priest as he went in with the sacrifices for the children of Israel so that they could be covered from one year to the next.

There is no flesh that can stand before God, so when the priest went in (and God allowed me to see him coming), an animal had to be slain just for this priest. And the blood of this calf had to be taken and had to be applied to the priest and put on all of the articles of the room where he went. But this priest could not begin his work in the holy place until something else happened.

Aaron, the high priest at that time, was told to take a handful of incense, incense that was a type of Jesus. That incense had been beaten— it had felt the scourge of suffering and pounding. And some live coals had to be taken off of the fire, which was a type of judgment. As Aaron entered into the holiest place where God was, he had to quickly put that handful of incense on the fire, on these live coals. And a cloud ascended from the incense. As the cloud went over the top and Aaron became engulfed in a cloud, a sweet-smelling incense reached up and pleased God Himself, and God then looked down and saw Aaron through the cloud which represented Jesus Christ and His suffering. Aaron could place the blood over the mercy seat and the other places in that holy place for himself and the people. Then, knowing that he was covered and knowing that God looked at him through the cloud, Aaron could bring the people to that place where they were covered.

God said, "You've got to do this or you're going to die, Aaron."

Aaron could only die for himself. God had provided a way whereby he could be accepted, but He said Jesus, the sinless Son of God, went in as the High Priest with no atonement for Himself. No covering. He went in before God, the sin-bearer, and the stroke of God's judgment and God's wrath penetrated Him and He became the real incense then as He took the stroke of God's wrath. And that incense ascended up and it covered all who would put their trust in Him. Everything in that tabernacle was a type of Jesus. But the most beautiful thing of all was Jesus becoming our covering through offering sweet-smelling incense unto God. So those who come to Him are covered.

Of course, we know that God didn't just cover our sins, He took them away. He showed that through the scapegoat, which was led out into the wilderness into a place where he could never be found. And that's what has happened to your sin. It's not only covered but it's removed. The Bible says that as far as the East is from the West, so far has He removed your transgression from you. And over the top is the covering of Jesus Christ. And so when God looks down at you, all of those things that happened in the normal course of this life are hidden. And you are accepted in Him. He only asks that you put your faith in what He has done for you.

I was allowed to see Jesus going into the presence of God with the blood to sprinkle. I've seen it from practically every angle, and my heart literally broke. But now I have a confidence in God that I've never had before.

You know, when the angel first came and told me to give this message about the blood covering to people, I hesitated because I had spent twenty-eight years in the community preaching the gospel and I didn't want to, in one night, destroy something that I had built up for so long. I didn't give the message right away. I knew that it wasn't going to be easy for people to accept the fact that I'd been visited by angels.

Three weeks after this first message from Gabriel, those same strong arms sat me up in bed and said, "You haven't given that message."

I felt that I was in trouble, but the angel said, "Your Father knows how you feel about this. He knows your concern, and He's going to help you." Then he gave me some more scripture. He told me the story in the first chapter of Luke of God's great love for families that He showed through John the Baptist. He said that through John the Baptist He would turn the hearts of the fathers back to the children and the children's hearts back to the fathers. Then He would take the rebellious generation and weave them back into the family and prove to them total forgiveness and restore them to a point of total innocence.

He (Gabriel) said the reason why so many young people cannot communicate with their parents is because their lives are completely filled with guilt. They have been ensnared and trapped by the rottenness and the stench of this old world, and they can't open up and talk about it with their parents.

But God is out to let them know that they do not have to carry this guilt anymore, and that His forgiveness is so complete that He will bring them to the wisdom of the just. He will help the wayward son or daughter comprehend and know what the full blessing of being justified really means. Do you see why I must share this message that I received?

Let's believe God's Word and His messenger—the guilt is gone and young and old alike are justified before God and reconciled back to Him. Glory!

Because the barriers are down now and the cloud is erased in between, the warm rays of God's love are now coming in. The term "shed abroad" is the same term for light. All of these are made available by His blood. He said we are not only justified, but we shall be saved from wrath through Him. This is a promise and an assurance that we are not only going to be saved here—not only has the enmity been destroyed—but we have assurance of what is going to happen tomorrow. We see that on judgment day, "For if when we were His enemies we were reconciled to God by the death of His Son, much more shall we be saved by His life." Underline the "much mores" in your Bible!

I would say one of the greatest problems that I hear about from people who come to see me is their fear that they might fall. Yet I tell you that the Lord is able to keep us from falling. Paul said that he discovered that if you believe, God gives this justification much more. Then he gave his reason for saying this. Paul reasoned that if God justified you when you were his enemy, when you didn't love God at all, when you were in a force that was opposing God, then God is capable of keeping you from falling now. If God justified you and picked you out when you had a gun pointed at Him, how much more now, when you're a member of His family, will you be saved by His life! As long as you know He's living there, He will keep you from falling. He won't keep you from falling if you want to fall. You can wrench yourself loose and fall. But He wants us to know that those who desire to live for God can rest in the assurance that He will not let us fall. Of course, the people who are having all these questions aren't people who want to quit living for God.

It's some of God's choicest believers who are filled with fear constantly, and God wants us to relax in Him. He said the blood was a gift of grace, meaning something we can't earn or merit, a special favor from God. He tells us because of the blood, because Jesus died for us, because of the sacrifice, we can receive the gift of His grace. Then because of the gift of grace we can have the ability to control our lives.

I realize that many people have up and down experiences in the Lord, but we don't have to have them. When we can understand our position in the Lord, we can have a life that is a life of victory. God would not be God if He wasn't able to provide us with a life of victory. So He tells us the basic thing that we need to have this life of victory is to deny ourselves. There are so many people who feel that their relationship with God is based on their ability to produce righteousness or goodness and to meet certain demands. They think, *If I could do this then I could have a life of victory, I'll be able to make it.* But that isn't what God says. God didn't say that those were the kind of people who would reign and have control in this life. He said the victorious are those who receive the abundance of grace, that free gift, and reach out and say, "God, I'm taking it. I didn't earn it, but You gave it to me anyway. Jesus, I'm taking that covering that You have for me, which is the atonement that is so real and rich." Grace does not happen because we work hard to receive it. The Bible says, "It's not of works lest any man should boast; it's by grace that you're saved." It's His grace, so when we accept that free gift of grace, this is something that grows, and spiritual victories are a product of accepting His righteousness first.

People often struggle with bondage. They stumble along with constant fear so that they're not able to have enough spiritual energy to produce what they want to produce. When they quit struggling and they just accept that free gift of His righteousness and start loving Jesus and drawing that strength that comes from Him, they begin to grow and they're able to kick the devil right out of the way.

One of the worst concepts that believers have is that Christ wants to reign in our lives. Indirectly, yes, that is true. But Christ says to you; "Let me put you in the driver's seat. You can reign—I've given you the power, I've given you the grace, and I've given you the righteousness."

When we see something coming we can say, "I have the power to overcome this thing." But when we feel like its God's job to do the driving and we fall, we may say, "I sure don't know why Christ didn't help me that time. I prayed and I asked the Lord, but I don't have any direction." Reigning comes about by the blood of Jesus. God wants to direct us, but He wants us in the driver's seat.

Because man was separated from God, he had to have reconciliation. Enmity had come. God said that the soul that sins shall die, and the very justice of God demands judgment on sin. So the wrath of God was there pulsating, striking out at sin, but the anger in God's heart was appeased by the blood of Christ, and the Word tells us now His anger is turned away from us. So we see that reconciliation is at the very heart of God's plan. It wasn't an afterthought; it started way back before the world ever began. We see it in the sacrifices, in the tabernacle, and in the feasts. In fact, this is the whole purpose of Jesus coming into the world!

> And, having made peace through the blood of his cross, by him to reconcile all things unto himself; by him, I say, whether they be things in earth, or things in heaven. And you, that were sometime alienated and enemies in your mind by wicked works, yet now hath he reconciled In the body of his flesh through death, to present you holy and unblameable and unreproveable in his sight (Colossians 1:20-22).

When the Lord took me into the throne room to let me see things the way He sees them, the first thing He did was to make me feel at ease so I didn't have to feel under strain. I didn't have to worry that He'd reprove me if I might say the wrong thing or look the wrong way with the wrong kind of expression. He let me know that I didn't have to worry, that He wasn't looking for something to reprove me for. I didn't have to feel I was walking on eggshells around Him and putting on a pious front.

God's plan for His people was to bring them to a place where nobody could lay a charge against them, and nobody could blame them for anything. And this is why it says in Romans 8 that God refuses to listen to any charge laid against His people. This is the unblameable part. There are a lot of things you do wrong, but God isn't going to listen to them. He refuses to accept any charges against you—you're unblameable. This was His plan, yet people have become so mixed up in reading the Bible and taking little bits and pieces that they miss the whole plan. God's plan for people right at the very beginning was to bring them to a point where there wouldn't be anything that they could blame man for.

Then He used another word: He didn't say that they would be unreproved, because that would be present tense. But those who have slipped their hands into His and want to walk with God are putting their faith in that blood. He said that we are unreprovable. That means we can look right up into God's face now. We might do some things and say some things, but the blood of Jesus keeps washing away. Sometimes we are aware of sin, but God can't find anything to reprove us for. We can find it and our family can find it, so God was very careful to add three little words—*in His sight*—not in people's sight. So don't go around and say, "I'm the most perfect guy around here." You and all of your friends know that you're blamable and you're reprovable and you need to get kicked in the seat of your pants to get moving sometimes. But because your faith is in the blood, He has a gift of grace and righteousness over us, and when He looks down at that gift of righteousness, which is imputed to us, you know what He's looking at. He's looking at the righteousness of Jesus, and He says, "I can't find anything to reprove, criticize, reprimand, or correct here."

God says we can have victory in this life, we can reign in this life, and we can be right on top because of the blood of Christ. Incredibly, the blood of Christ not only does something between us and Him, but the blood then begins another work under this covering. Later on in this book we'll look at sanctification, how underneath this wonderful covering the blood sanctifies and cleanses. He does a work that helps us to minister to people and to let people see what's happening underneath the covering. The blood doesn't just stop working there, but we have to know that reconciliation exists before we can embrace any other work of the blood. We can try any method we want to, but if we haven't taken the free covering that God puts over the top, we are working from the wrong end.

In Ephesians 1:4 we are told that God's plan for us before He even made the world was that we would be holy and without blame—not before the world but before Him. Our problem is that we look at how we see ourselves, we look at how people see us, and then we project that up to God and say, "God, look at me and all my failures and everything else." God wants us to know that we can look up at God's face unreprovable!

There's another word, the word propitiation, which means reconciliation for our sins. The blood is given to reconcile us or bring us in holiness back to God.

> For sin shall not have dominion over you: for ye are not under
> the law, but under grace (Romans 6:14).

What joy! He removes the power of sin! We often think that it's still there, but because of faith in the blood of Jesus, the power of sin and even the guilt of sin is removed. Through the blood of His cross the guilt is gone, and we can look up into His face and say, "Ah, thank you, Jesus, it's gone." The barrier of God's wrath is removed!

> Much more then, being now justified by his blood, we shall be
> saved from wrath through him (Romans 5:9).

Our sin erected a barrier between us and God and made us God's enemies instead of His family. God removed the barrier, and the very God we angered reaches down and saves us through the precious blood of His only Son. We are saved from wrath! His love and His wrath join hands. His wrath destroys and consumes the separating barrier. Because God is a just God, He could not justify us while sin was still there, so there has to be love and the wrath together. His wrath destroys and consumes sin, because wrath has to fall on sin and disobedience. And when Jesus took on Himself the sins of the whole world, the wrath of God reached out and darted forth and struck that sin. Jesus took the full charge there because of our sins that were on His life.

So this is why Paul could say, "I could still be just and the justifier of the one who puts his faith in the blood of Jesus." God's wrath is still there for sin, but He justifies that person because God's wrath sees the blood (and knows judgment has already struck), and that wrath turns around and hides in the love of God. Don't fear His wrath today. When your faith is in the blood, the wrath of God cannot penetrate because it has already spent its charge on sin.

The fourth thing on the blood is the removal of remembrance of sin. God has taken care of it. He removes the power of sin, He removes the guilt of sin, He removes the barrier between us and God. Now He removes even the remembrance of sin from His memory. "I have blotted it out," He states. It's gone from His memory. You can stand before God and say, "God, you remember this and this about me? I'm so glad you took care of that." God will just have to look at you and say, "I can't remember a thing about it." He removes the remembrance of sin.

We shall be saved from wrath through Him. Reconciliation is made up of three Greek words: Helios, which means *to make cheerful, to remove the reason for gloom, to lift the fallen countenance, to cover sin, to find God gracious and merciful.* Then the last of that word is *to avert calamity, because the world is heading towards judgment.* Through the blood we are restored to divine favor or the original position with God. To restore means *to put back in its original condition.* So this word restore means that Jesus brought back to people that blessed life which was in such fellowship and such peace where they could walk with God and talk with God and have wonderful fellowship as they did in the garden.

So when is reconciliation complete? It is when a man or woman is restored into a place where he or she can slip a hand into God's and say, "Let's go for a walk!"

As we walk along with Him, we can know that we are unblamable and unreprovable in His sight and don't have to worry about the situation we are in because we can't hide from Him anyway. He can look right smack through us. He knows all that's there, so there is no point in being anything but ourselves. But when we are with Him, we are in the safest place there is in the whole universe.

This is the heart of the Bible—it's the heart of His whole plan.

> Therefore if any man be in Christ, he is a new creature: old things are passed away; behold, all things are become new. [18]And all things are of God, who hath reconciled us to himself by Jesus Christ, and hath given to us the ministry of reconciliation (2 Corinthians 5:17-18).

When we have been reconciled, then He says, "I want you to go out there and apply this to some other people and let them know how real it is."

He's given unto us the ministry of reconciliation—of taking the barrier down, of taking people's hands and linking them with God, and letting them know the goodness of God. He's given us the ministry of reconciling sinners, not accusing, blaming, or reproving sinners for their sins. God committed unto us the word of reconciliation. God says, "You tell them that I'll do it, and I'll back you up. And I'll do it." That's the word of reconciliation. So because of this, we become His voice.

> Now then we are ambassadors for Christ, as though God did beseech you by us: we pray you in Christ's stead, be ye reconciled to God (2 Corinthians 5:20).

This is the word of reconciliation! "Be ye reconciled to God!" Now people need to know what it is—they need to see "reconciliation" written all over us. They need to see the lack of fear and the abundance of joy. They need to see the relaxation rubbed all over our faces. And then we can say, "Here, have a bite, praise God!" And He tells us why He has made Christ to be sin. He took the full stroke of God's judgment for sin so that we would be made the righteousness of God in Him.

I'll tell you, God is so wonderful! Don't allow any fear to come into your mind. Place your faith and trust in what Jesus has done and enjoy a new life of victory over sin!

Chapter Five

THE CLEANSING POWER OF THE BLOOD

THE IMPORTANCE OF the blood in God's plan of salvation is seen most clearly in the simple fact that there are more than seven hundred references to it in the Holy Bible. The blood was never far from God's heart, and it became the key factor in all of His dealings with man. The purpose and power of His blood takes on added meaning by a comparison with human blood. When I started reading about the power of the blood and analyzing the purposes and the power of the blood and the human life, I could just picture God when He was laying His plans and said, "How shall we make blood? Well, let's weave into the blood my story of redemption. Let's weave into it the story of the blood of Jesus."

The blood in your system carries nourishment to every cell in your body—nourishment your body needs in order to live. Your blood makes a full circuit once every twenty three seconds. You don't have to turn on a switch and say, "Now heart, start beating." It's going to beat whether you're awake or asleep. It just keeps on doing its job. And as you put your faith in Christ, the blood of Jesus Christ keeps bringing life to every cell in the body of Christ. There's enough of this cleansing, life-giving flow for every individual, for every little cell. And it's the blood of Christ that ties us together.

We are made of one blood, and we are all blood brothers and sisters in Christ. Wastes and poisons are carried off as this blood flows through our being. Those things that may attach themselves to us are dislodged and carried away by the built-in cleansing system that God made for our bodies. His blood keeps flowing while we're in fellowship and in harmony with Him, taking care of those things that would destroy or hurt.

This blood also protects us. Did you know that we have within our veins a silent army of soldiers ready to attack anything that would try to bring infection into our bodies? They're called white corpuscles. When you cut yourself, an infection would begin immediately, except that these "soldiers" are summoned to duty, and they head throughout your system to protect you and to ward off and fight off the infection. The blood of Jesus Christ has been given to us to ward off any attack of the enemy. The Lord wrote His redemption story in the science of our natural blood.

The blood will also defend against disease. They tell me that you can become immune to certain types of diseases by having a little bit of the blood turned into serum—blood from someone who has been attacked by the disease. If you have that injected into your veins, it causes you to be immune. Now here's a striking picture. Jesus Christ was smitten with a curse of sin. The Word tells us that God made Him to be sin for us, and He took the full force of God's judgment. Now His blood injected into us by the hand of God creates an immunity from judgment. Hallelujah! He took the full force of it. You've had an inoculation! They call these antibodies—a little substance that provides immunity.

Just think of the fact that there is a constant cleansing every twenty-three seconds going through your system. Every cell in your body is tied together by this life. Now in justification God covers your life. Some people have started from the other end and have thought that God wants us to make ourselves clean and to lay aside these various things that hurt us. For some reason or another, people like to struggle so that they feel that there's something they're doing or accomplishing in order to become clean. But that's starting at the wrong end. We can never make ourselves good enough for God.

As I explained earlier, the first thing that has to happen before we receive anything is to have the wrath of God appeased. So when God sees that blood, His wrath is turned away. But then He said, "I'm not through working with you only by justification." Justification is one of the most marvelous messages in the whole Bible, but God isn't finished after justification. He covers us with that blood, and then He designs the blood to flow through us underneath this covering. The things that have ruined our life—the pollution of sin and broken relationships—are all taken care of by the blood of Jesus Christ, which cleanses us as we walk with Him.

That blood that was shed *for* us is put *within* us and is working *through* us. It doesn't just make a life of misery bearable—it brings metamorphosis to us through and through. It makes us like Jesus!

That's why Paul could say that God's ultimate plan was that Jesus was made sin for us, sin clear through. He was made sin for us that we might not only be covered with righteousness but so that we might be made the righteousness of God in Him. This is because of His blood flowing through. The blood of Adam flowing through us had the seeds of death in it, and it was corruptible, but the blood of Jesus has the seeds of life that destroy the seeds of death. This is why we can say when we accept Jesus Christ we have eternal life; it doesn't mean that we won't have a time of transition from one area of life to another. God doesn't consider the cessation of breathing and the activities of this life an end at all. Life to Him is on both sides of the river. Jesus Himself said, "God isn't the God of the dead, He's the God of the living." He's the God of Abraham, and Abraham is alive. He's the God of Jacob and Isaac, and they're still alive, they're just on the other side of the river. And those loved ones of yours who are gone, they're not dead. He's their God, and He said, "I'm not the God of the dead but of the living." I believe those loved ones over there have a pretty good idea of what you're doing over here, because the Spirit can carry them the word and the message. There are a couple portions of scripture that talk about examples of this. God doesn't want us probing too deep in this area; otherwise, He would have put more of it in the Bible. But He gave us just enough.

In reconciliation the barrier was destroyed, and God's wrath was appeased. In justification the records were destroyed, and, in cleansing, the pollution or the seeds of sin and death are destroyed. In justification God hides sin from His sight, in cleansing He takes it away.

> That which was from the beginning, which we have heard, which we have seen with our eyes, which we have looked upon, and our hands have handled, of the Word of life; (For the life was manifested, and we have seen it, and bear witness, and shew unto you that eternal life, which was with the Father, and was manifested unto us;) That which we have seen and heard declare we unto you, that ye also may have fellowship with us: and truly our fellowship is with the Father, and with his Son Jesus Christ. And these things write we unto you, that your joy may be full. This then is the message which we have heard of him, and declare unto you, that God is light, and in him is no darkness at all. If we say that we have fellowship with him, and walk in darkness, we lie, and do not the truth: But if we walk in the light, as he is in the light, we have fellowship one with another, and the blood of Jesus Christ his Son cleanseth us from all sin. If we say that we have no sin, we deceive ourselves, and the truth is not in us. If we confess our sins, he is faithful and just to forgive us our sins, and to cleanse us from all unrighteousness (1 John 1:1-9).

In fitting into God's plan and making it work, I like that verse over in Isaiah 1:18: "Come now, let us reason together, says the Lord; let's talk about this thing. Though your sins are as scarlet, they shall be white as snow." This is God's plan, this is His call. People who are weighed down with sin may wonder how this can happen; I've talked with many of them. Down inside they hunger to please God, and their heart's desire is to be free from the thing that is dragging them down.

Christians who are failing to live victorious lives have the same thing. Probably more than any other request that comes is to be free from something that is hurting them and dragging them down. God tells us what to do. He says, "You can come now, my wrath is turned away and you can come and talk to Me about it. Come now and let us reason together, I'll take care of all that." He does it by the cleansing blood. He takes care of it; then living in fellowship. Let's take a look at verse nine. If we confess our sins, so through confession we can have this fellowship. If we confess our sins, He is faithful and just to forgive us of our sins. That's justification, and to cleanse us from all unrighteousness speaks of the cleansing happening within us. In l John 1:7 it speaks about living in fellowship with the Lord. In all evangelical schools and from the pulpits of many evangelical churches and many others, it is preached that our relationship with God hinges on the amount of light He has given us. So this statement is made, "That person isn't walking in the light that he has, and here's a person who has all kinds of light and knows all kinds of things about the Bible, so she has a lot more to walk in."

That night when God dealt with me, He put his thumb right on that in a blazing magnification on this verse. He said, "What do you believe, how do you interpret this verse, how have you been preaching it?" I explained to the Lord that in all the other commentaries that was how it was said. Much evangelical teaching is not based on revelation from God or from enlightenment from His Word, but it's on a lack of definite direction from God, and they have tried to do what they could. When I said it's walking in all the light of knowledge that you have, the Lord said, "Do you walk in all of the light that you have?" I said, "No, God, I've really missed the boat an awful lot." Then He said, "If your cleansing is dependent on your walking in the light and you are not walking in all the light, how can you expect to have any cleansing?" He also asked me, "If you do walk in the light, do you walk in it like Jesus walked in it?" And I said, "No, you know I don't." And He said, "Do you know anybody who does?" I said "No, I never met anybody who did." And He said, "Then nobody is going to be saved, nobody is going to receive any cleansing."

Do you know what the Lord did then? He lifted my eyes, and He said, "Let Me show you what light is. It's not knowledge; if it was based on knowledge, then you would be earning your cleansing. You'd be earning your fellowship, but this is something you can't earn. It's by grace that you've been saved." And I could see it blazing then in verse five, "This then is the message that God is light. He lights every man who comes into the world. And that light is life; God is light." And then he goes on to say because God is light, He's shining out and lighting people, and as long as you walk in this fellowship with Him, walk close enough so you can say, "Hi, God," and know that He's there and have that fellowship, he said, "The blood of Jesus Christ cleanses," it flows just as far as His light does. The blood flows as far as His fellowship. It flows as far as His light comes in His fellowship. And the blood flows the same distance.

In this plane, walking in this light, it is impossible to sin, according to some because of sanctification — you may make some mistakes, but you don't sin. But that isn't what God said. God said that while you are walking in this light, there's going to be some sin that will overtake you, and some of you are going to sin. I don't want you to, but you can sin and still be in this plane." The reason why, and He had this verse, that blood is flowing there is so that sin may overtake you or blight your life, but the blood keeps on flowing and keeps on washing it away. That word cleanses in John is present tense. The blood of Jesus Christ, God's Son, cleanses us from all sin. If we walk in fellowship with Jesus, we don't have to walk around with our heads bowed down in fear wondering whether or not we are going to make it when Jesus comes. If we stay in fellowship with Him, all of hell can't take us away because God has a built-in cleansing agent there. It's all mixed in with His light and with His fellowship. There may be some thoughts that come into your mind that you know displease God, but the blood just keeps on cleansing. You may lift your voice and get mad at someone, but the blood just keeps on cleansing.

> "This then is the message that we have heard of Him, that God is light" (1 John 1:5).

God is cleansing, God is our fellowship. If we sin, we have an advocate with the Father, Jesus Christ the righteous. He said that He has become the propitiation. That's a person becoming a propitiation. That word propitiation is the same word translated as mercy seat. So when you read about the mercy seat that God has put there in the throne of grace, in the tabernacle of worship, it is a golden lid, something of tremendous value. Underneath the mercy seat is the Ark of the Covenant. Inside of the Ark of the Covenant are all of the broken laws of God signifying all of the sins and the guilt and the transgression put under the propitiation, this golden covering. Then God said, "Now take the blood just to make this a true picture. Take two goats, kill one of them and take the blood of one of these goats and sprinkle it over the top of this mercy seat. You want to come and make contact with Me. There's only one place in the whole universe that I'll meet with you, only one place, and that's the door that the blood has opened." That's the power of this cleansing blood. God said when you come now to this mercy seat and you identify yourself with that, there will I meet with you, and I'll talk with you over the cherubim. So there is a spot where the sin is covered.

Now the beautiful picture of this is God said not only is He the propitiation and covering for our sin, but underneath the blood of Jesus is doing a continual, constant cleansing work also. This mercy seat has the covering for the sin, and God accepts the sinner. That's the covering that we talked about over the top. Picture that blood covering over you in the

Spirit right now. Be free. But inside of the ark there are still the remains of the broken laws, so now God says take this other goat; it took two animals to fully make God's picture. He said to take the believer and put his hands on this goat so that he could be identified with this goat and pronounce the sins of this person upon this goat and then take this goat out into the wilderness to a place where he could never be found. When you have put your faith in the blood and it's covered, God has said, "Now that it's covered, we will take it all away." He's working right underneath that covering, and He's removing the sins far away where they can never be found again.

When God took sin away, He really took it away. Reading in 1 Peter, "Forasmuch as you know you were not redeemed with corruptible things but with the precious blood of Christ, who was the Lamb of God without blemish or without spot. You were redeemed through the incorruptible blood of Jesus. You weren't saved with corruptible things, but you were saved with incorruptible." That word incorruptible means it can never pass away, it can never lose its power, and it can never be destroyed. The blood that flowed from Jesus' back, that blood that was shed did not stay in the ground and become corruptible and become mixed with the corruption with this earth. That blood is incorruptible; [ ] every drop of that blood was saved and taken to heaven. That blood is still there. So when Paul had a glimpse of heaven, there was God the Father of all, there was Jesus, there were the spirits of just men made perfect, and there was an innumerable company of angels. And he said, "By the way, there's the blood— it's still there." He let John have a look in Revelation. And He said there's the blood, it's still there. As the animal in the Old Testament was slain, every drop of blood had to be caught, not one drop was allowed to be lost, and God was giving them a picture here that with Jesus, His blood, these were just types of His blood. God says it's got to be so exact because not one drop is going to be wasted. It's incorruptible, it can't be destroyed, and it avails for sin forever.

There's plenty of cleansing for everybody. There's enough immunity in the blood that God applies to our life to ward off spiritual sickness. There's enough to warm our life, there's enough to feed us, to protect us. The blood has never lost its power. And in that injection, the corruptible is injected with the incorruptible, the seeds of death have been destroyed with the seeds of life.

Chapter Six

THE BLOOD that SANCTIFIES

W<small>E HAVE SEEN</small> the power of the blood of Jesus at work in justification, in cleansing and reconciliation. In this chapter we will see how the blood of Jesus brings life continually to the one who has been reconciled and cleansed—contrary to accepted teachings that sanctification has to do with the absence of sin and the destroying of the old nature and so forth. The blood of Jesus brings the very life, beauty, purpose, and provision of Jesus to the believer. As we explore these Bible truths, keep your heart and mind open, for this could be the greatest revelation of your life. We will consider what sanctification is, the agents used to activate sanctification, and the results of the work of sanctification through the blood of Jesus. Let's look at what God's Word has to say about the blood:

> But Christ being come an high priest of good things to come, by a greater and more perfect tabernacle, not made with hands, that is to say, not of this building; Neither by the blood of goats and calves, but by his own blood he entered in once into the holy place, having obtained eternal redemption for us. For if the blood of bulls and of goats, and the ashes of an heifer

sprinkling the unclean, sanctifieth to the purifying of the flesh: How much more shall the blood of Christ, who through the eternal Spirit offered himself without spot to God, purge your conscience from dead works to serve the living God? And for this cause he is the mediator of the new testament, that by means of death, for the redemption of the transgressions that were under the first testament, they which are called might receive the promise of eternal inheritance (Hebrews 9:11-15).

This teaching on the power of the blood came directly from the heart of God. God, let me see the blood as a mighty river flowing. And as it flowed from God's heart across the arena of human experience, there was a great big barrier in the way—a barrier of sin. But when Jesus died, the dam broke, and that mighty river of the blood and life of Jesus flowed and swept away the barrier. *This was our reconciliation to God by the blood of His Son, Jesus.*

God records everything that happens in the human life. Those records that were against us, the Word tells us, were washed away by the flow of the river into God's sea of forgetfulness, never to be remembered against us anymore forever—every record gone. *That's justification by blood.*

And then as that river washes away the records of sin written in the human life, that mighty river flows on and destroys the pollution of sin—*that's the cleansing by the blood.*

The cleansing is not the sanctification. Sanctification comes after the cleansing. When the Word says the blood works for our sanctification, it is saying that the power of the blood (or all of the power of heaven) is adapted to human life and use.

You know there are great transformers around carrying electricity. But before they can come in here and light the room, they have to be converted into a way that they could be used here. It's the same way in the power of the blood.

God asked me, "What is the power of the blood?" God let me see that the power of the blood was measured by the life of that one it flowed through. The value of that blood is determined by the value of that life. And the Word tells us that in Him was all the fullness of God. So when you think of the power of the blood, what you're actually recognizing is the power of heaven and the authority of the universe that swept away the barrier, destroyed the records, wiped out the pollution, and now brings us the fullness of God Himself—the very life of Jesus.

What is sanctification? It is the sharing of Jesus' life in our mortal bodies. The life of Jesus is so much more important to us. He didn't want to point us to the dark day but the bright day of His life. It is possible for the believer to be so involved with the dark side of the cross, which was Jesus' side, that we fail to see the bright side of the cross, which is our side.

> For this is the will of God, even your sanctification, that ye should abstain from fornication (1 Thessalonians 4:3).

Life is in the blood. In the blood of Jesus dwelt all of the fullness of God, and we are being filled with all of the fullness of God. So Jesus gives us His blood and life to flow through us. God has blessed us with all spiritual blessings in heavenly places. When the life of Jesus flows through the life of believers, there are times when they are in heavenly places. So He has raised us up with Him to sit in heavenly places.

When that river flows and the life of Jesus touches the human body, the glory of God touches that life. God's glory is the pulsating atmosphere that comes from the throne of God. As that sanctifying river flows, it makes available the life of Jesus, and the glory comes. The glory actually activates all of the wonderful life of Jesus. The glory of God actually sanctifies the life of a believer.

So sanctification is actually adapting to the life force of Jesus. The truth, faith, and the Holy Spirit will open up the floodgates and cause Jesus' life to flow. Faith activates the blood of Jesus. The Spirit keeps the river flowing. Jesus sanctifies us. The life of Jesus begins to flow through the name of Jesus. When I am speaking in a meeting, even as I have people begin to say that name, His life begins to flow.

> Elect according to the foreknowledge of God the Father, through sanctification of the Spirit, unto obedience and sprinkling of the blood of Jesus Christ: Grace unto you, and peace, be multiplied (1 Peter 1:2).

Even God's peace comes through the sanctifying work of the blood of Jesus! You can't really have peace until you quit struggling. You can't really relax until you realize that God is taking care of those things that could bother you. Grace and peace are ours because of the wonderful flow of God. All of these things are brought about by His blood. His life in us brings the cloud of glory!

Chapter Seven

THE BLOOD REMOVES THE DISTANCE AND BRINGS US NEAR TO GOD

I N THIS CHAPTER I want to talk about the power of the blood of Christ to bring us closer to God.

First, I want to share a beautiful truth that the Lord made so real to me early one Sunday morning as the angel Gabriel met with me in my office and spoke to me about what God is doing—more specifically, about the seeds that have been sown in the hearts of people around the world. He said that the gospel message may not have been received—it may not have germinated. The seed goes forth again and again, and it has been sown in many, many, many lives. God's plan for believers is that we take on His light and become the light of God to these people. His plan is that we actually partake of the nature of Jesus.

He doesn't necessarily want you to become the greatest Bible teacher in the earth. He didn't intend for you just to grow in great stature. He wants you to be like Jesus. In a nutshell, 2 Peter 1 is God's plan for you. Let's look at some of this scripture:

Grace and peace be multiplied unto you through the knowledge of God and of Jesus our Lord, who according to His
divine power has given to us all things that pertain unto life
and godliness through the knowledge of Him that has called
us unto glory and virtue. All things that pertain to this life,
which pertains to godliness, have been given to us when we
learn to know Him, see Him as He is. Whereby given unto
us exceeding great and precious promises that by these you
might be partakers of the divine nature, having escaped the
pollution or the corruption that is in the world through lust
(2 Peter 1:2-4).

God wants you to be like Jesus, partaker of that divine nature. In order
to be like Jesus, we need to have an escape plan from sin. God set up a
beautiful escape plan! Those things that you have been battling will fall
away and you'll have victory over them in the beauty of Jesus. God wants
literally millions of representatives of the beauty of Jesus in this world.

And beside this, giving all diligence, add to your faith virtue;
and to virtue knowledge; And to knowledge temperance;
and to temperance patience; and to patience godliness; And
to godliness brotherly kindness; and to brotherly kindness
charity (2 Peter 1:5-7).

All of these things are the characteristics of the nature of Jesus, and
He will add these things to your life.

For if these things be in you, and abound, they make you that
ye shall neither be barren nor unfruitful in the knowledge
of our Lord Jesus Christ. But he that lacketh these things is
blind, and cannot see afar off, and hath forgotten that he was
purged from his old sins. Wherefore the rather, brethren, give
diligence to make your calling and election sure: for if ye do
these things, ye shall never fall. For so an entrance shall be

ministered unto you abundantly into the everlasting kingdom of our Lord and Saviour Jesus Christ. Wherefore I will not be negligent to put you always in remembrance of these things, though ye know them, and be established in the present truth (2 Peter 1:8-12).

God's desire for you is for you to be like Jesus and not to slip back into an old way.

Now, let's return to the thought that this world is a great field that's been planted. Seeds have been sown. Often, in many places they've been watered by the tears of people. God's great work that He's doing today is to draw people close to Himself and lead them into a place where His life is seen in them—Jesus' life is light. The Word tells us that in Him was life, and that life was the light of men, and it now lights up the people in the world. So look at it this way: God has set you in the world as a light and now He says, "It's time for you to arise and shine, for your light has come, and the glory of the Lord has risen upon you."

The looks, the nature, the glory of Jesus has risen in you and is streaming from you. What is the purpose of this? To give you a place of beauty and of prominence? No. That likeness of Jesus that's streaming from your life becomes the warm rays of God's love, of His gentleness, of His nature that goes forth.

As this mighty angel was speaking to me that morning, he said that the seed had been sown and, as we partake of the nature of Jesus, we shine, and the warm rays from our life will cause a germinating of the sown seed. All over the country there's going to be life springing forth because the seed of the gospel is there. He doesn't say to stop sowing, but He does say that as we move about in this world, as we live and minister among people, that something inside their hearts will come to life!

Hallelujah! The seed is going to spring to life.

Perhaps you are reading this book and you do not yet know Christ. I want you to think of times that the seed of knowing Christ has been sown in your life. Perhaps you've been in a home and saw a mother or a father who loved God. Or you've been out working and you've looked up into the sky and your mind seemed to drift to the things of God—*there must be a God out there somewhere!* Or perhaps there was a time when you were spared a grievous accident by God's help. Or you were listening to the radio and you heard a song that told about God and there was a softness in your heart. You may have even had to dab a tear away from your eye as a seed was sown and your heart was touched. You may have heard a message sometime a long time ago, and a seed was sown.

I have to tell you right now, God is carrying the message to you, He's saying, "I want you, I love you." Do you want Him? Why don't you just stop right now and tell Him. Tell Him that you want Him, you believe that Jesus is the Son of God who died for your sins, and ask Him to come into your life and make you new. This is the most important decision you could ever make in your whole life. Come to Him now. He wants you. He loves you. He's waiting.

And after you invite Jesus to live inside of you, He wants the world to be loved through you, through the beauty of Jesus. Oh, Jesus! I feel that God is here (even as you read this page) in such a powerful way. I feel that He's putting His hand on your life. What seed has been sown in you? Not only the gospel seed, but seeds of hope, seeds of desire for service for God, seeds of real faith and belief are being warmed right now in your heart by the warmth of His light in your heart. Do you feel a quickening in your own spirit? Oh, the quickening of the Holy Spirit! Hallelujah!

I think of this telephone call that we received from up in river country. A man called me, weeping, and told me he'd listened to a recording of me talking about the seeds that are sown in our lives. He was actually listening to the recording in a saloon! He said that sixteen years ago he heard a sermon and felt that he should surrender to the Lord, and as he listened to the recording of me speaking, it all came back to him. So he called and asked me how he could find Jesus. I was able to pray for him over the phone, and he slipped his hand into the Lord's at that time.

Do you know what he said? He said, "Now I'm going back to the saloon and I'm going to tell the other sixteen men who were weeping as they were listening to that recording how to find Jesus." Praise God!

I wish I could communicate this to you the way Gabriel communicated it to me that day in my office, the way it was communicated to my own heart. There are seeds already planted in people's hearts, seeds that are ready to spring forth as the light of God's love shines upon them. As he was talking to me about this, something happened that I will never forget—I felt so awed by it, I couldn't even talk about it in church. But while Gabriel was speaking to me, suddenly a shaft of light about eighteen inches across came into that home office. It did not diffuse and go out into the room; it stayed together like a blue-white pipe. It was a shaft of light. I looked at it, but it was so dazzling I couldn't keep my eyes upon it, and I felt so absolutely consumed by the brightness of that light. Gabriel, who was standing by me, stopped talking. The other angel that was there with us stopped. The light stayed for about five minutes. It was stunning! The angels told me at that point about the warmth of that light and how it germinated the seeds of life.

Oh, God, have I taken this? Has this been important enough to me? How important this must be to God that by supernatural means He let me know that He wants His believers to be shafts of light beaming warmth, love, and kindness into the world. He wants us to grasp the truth that the seeds that are sown in lives everywhere will suddenly germinate and people will say, "Oh, I need God! I want Him—I must have Him!"

What is God trying to do? God loves people. God is not seeking to condemn people; He's seeking to bring them to Himself. And Jesus, when He stated what He came to do, He said, "I have come that they might have life and that they might have it more abundantly" (John 10:10). Praise God!

The death of Christ opened up a mighty river of life from God's heart to man. So far, we've learned these applications of the blood of Jesus to our lives:

- The blood destroyed the separating barrier—reconciliation
- The blood erased the records of all charges against us—justification
- The blood removed the inner pollution in men's lives—cleansing
- The blood brings life, vigor, and happiness—sanctification

In this chapter we will see that the river of life carries us into the very presence of God, removing all distance and providing fellowship through the blood of Jesus. We will consider our right to stand before Him, the results of living in His presence, and what it means to minister in His presence. In the course of the flow of this river, you will find that all barriers between God and people are swept away.

The flow of this river removes the records as we put our faith in the blood, so that God cannot remember the sins committed. He not only forgets your sin, He forgets. He has forgiven you. So you can't say, "God, I thank you for the seventy times you forgave me."

God says, "What seventy times?" His forgiveness is so complete.

Then there's the beautiful story of sanctification we talked about in the previous chapter, which is not cleansing or eternal life but is the actual life of Jesus being felt in our mortal bodies—His incorruptible life. The blood that fell from His brow, the blood that came from His side, His hands, and His back, the blood that may have fallen and dropped along the way—not one drop of that blood was wasted or just went into the soil and was corrupted.

> Being born again, not of corruptible seed, but of incorruptible, by the word of God, which liveth and abideth for ever (1 Peter 1:23).

The Word tells us that His blood, because it contained all of the fullness of God Himself, was preserved because it is incorruptible. It can never be destroyed.

John had a chance to visit heaven, and he said, "There it is, there's the blood of Jesus—still there."

As the ages of eternity roll on, the blood that purchased us and does its cleansing just continues on and on and on. Paul had a chance to see it. Did you know that Paul was caught up and had a chance to visit in the heavens?

> But ye are come unto mount Sion, and unto the city of the living God, the heavenly Jerusalem, and to an innumerable company of angels, To the general assembly and church of the firstborn, which are written in heaven, and to God the Judge of all, and to the spirits of just men made perfect, And to Jesus the mediator of the new covenant, and to the blood of sprinkling, that speaketh better things than that of Abel (Hebrews 12:22-24).

There it is. There is the blood, and it is still speaking, and it is still saying, "Count that person just—she has put her faith and her trust in Me." Hallelujah, the blood is there.

When people feel the flow of His life, the old burden lifts, their eyes shine, and radiation begins to come out of their faces. They can move out in a victory they never had before, kicking the enemy out of the way. When I see this, I realize that Jesus adapted the power of the universe that is in the blood to human life. The life of Jesus was being felt in those mortal bodies. As we studied in the last chapter, when God spoke of sanctification, this is what He was talking about—the application of the life of the Godhead into the human life. It's not a cold, fearful force but a little bit of that atmosphere of heaven that shines through when God's glory is revealed and every person who drinks of that life becomes a reflection of what heaven is really like. It's not a hard thing, it's not an unhappy thing, and it's not a pious thing. What God is doing today is making His people like Jesus.

The blood has purchased for us a wonderful fellowship with God.

> That which was from the beginning, which we have heard, which we have seen with our eyes, which we have looked upon, and our hands have handled, of the Word of life; (For the life was manifested, and we have seen it, and bear witness, and shew unto you that eternal life, which was with the Father, and was manifested unto us;) That which we have seen and heard declare we unto you, that ye also may have fellowship with us: and truly our fellowship is with the Father, and with his Son Jesus Christ. ⁴And these things write we unto you, that your joy may be full. ⁵This then is the message which we have heard of him, and declare unto you, that God is light, and in him is no darkness at all (1 John 1:1-5).

People come with their heaviness and darkness of spirit, and they look unto Him and they are lightened, drawing from that beautiful light that comes from heaven that brings fellowship. In Him there is no darkness at all.

> If we say that we have fellowship with him, and walk in darkness, we lie, and do not the truth: But if we walk in the light, as he is in the light, we have fellowship one with another, and the blood of Jesus Christ his Son cleanseth us from all sin (1 John 1:6-7).

When we are walking in this type of fellowship, the blood of Jesus Christ cleanses us from all sin. It just keeps right on cleansing. Some folks have taught that when you are in this place of fellowship and sanctification, there is no sin that can come. But that's not so. The Word lets us know that there may be definite sin each day. There may be sin in thought or in word. There may be some things that you have practically defied God on, but the hunger and desire in your heart is to walk with Him and serve Him.

You are already cleansed when you start the day because of His blood. When you have laid everything out before God, you are cleansed. As you walk in this wonderful light, all sin is gone. You don't have to wrestle and struggle and be so concerned. The main thing for you to be concerned about is loving Jesus and looking unto Him. I know a man who was struggling to try to please the Lord to the point that he almost lost his mind. He felt that practically twenty four hours a day he had to be on his knees. He would say half a sentence and then say, "Oh God, I want your holiness, and I want your sanctification!" He did that until he was a nervous wreck.

I told that fellow, "I don't even want you to read the Bible or quote the Bible. The enemy is using everything that you have learned there to whip you in the ground."

If you remember, the enemy tried to use the scripture on Christ, too. God has saved you, He has written your name down in heaven, and He wants you to know it. But He wants you to develop not just a big fat spirit constantly concerned about keeping the flesh dead and humanity non-existent. God intends for you to be well-rounded in spirit, soul, and body. If you don't take care of these other areas, your spirit is not going to be worth two cents. So I gave him a *National Geographic* magazine. I said, "I want you to read through that, and I want you to report on it."

Then he took two or three days, and he called and said, "I've read through the *Geographic* and I read through the *Reader's Digest* you gave me. I learned some interesting things about those coal mines." For the first time in a long time he was relaxed because his soul was beginning to be restored.

He was told what God expected of him, and he was raised in a setting where eight hours a day they try to program their people so that there's such a tension in their minds and struggling about what they have to do that they are trying to get some handholds on a steep cliff trying to reach where God is located. Each time they make a few inches they slide back a foot, and there's a constant feeling of failure. I told him I wanted him to let the Spirit lift him up. I warned him that it would take a little bit of time to get rid of the rituals and traditions that tied him up in bondage.

I can't understand people being so down and feeling like it's such a hardship to walk with God, when it can be such a wonderful thing. You can be so happy, be yourself, and be the person that God created you to be! You can pull the mask away and come forth and be yourself in the Lord! He would have made you some other way if He wanted you some other way. But he doesn't want everybody to be just a whole bunch of rubber stamps. He made us all different because He likes us that way.

When you are way off from God He doesn't say, "If you'll take some steps here and come a little bit closer and do this and follow this guide-book until you get right there, then I'll listen to you." On the contrary, He says, "If you call unto Me from the farthest point away, I'll remove the distance by my miracle power."

It reminds me of when the disciples were out in the boat, and they were toiling there. But when they called upon Jesus, He came into the boat, quieted things down, and immediately they arrived at their desti-nation. He just caused the distance to disappear. He has this ability.

> But now in Christ Jesus ye who sometimes were far off are
> made nigh by the blood of Christ (Ephesians 2:13).

I still remember the excitement I had when the Lord made this verse so real to me, when I saw the distance just melt. You were far off but you are made nigh by the blood of Jesus.

> Having therefore, brethren, boldness to enter into the holiest
> by the blood of Jesus (Hebrews 10:19).

Hebrews is one of my most favorite books in the whole Bible because God gives the pattern of what's going on in heaven all the time in this book. The whole gospel is in here; God's whole plan is seen in operation in this book. Let's look at verse sixteen:

> This is the covenant that I will make with them after those days, saith the Lord, I will put my laws into their hearts, and in their minds will I write them; And their sins and iniquities will I remember no more (Hebrews 10:16-17).

There's no more offering for sin. Because of this you can get real bold.

People down through the centuries weren't able to approach God. There had to be a fear because if they did one thing wrong their lives would be taken. They had to come with such fear knowing that everything had to be perfect, because it was a prototype of what Jesus would do in making us perfect before God. But now Paul was saying all of this carefulness is gone because the cake has already been made, it's already frosted, and it's not going to fall. You know how you have to walk around in your kitchen when a cake made from scratch is rising? If you stomp or one of the children jumps hard, your cake could flop in the oven, and it won't rise again. Some of you ladies know this. You have to be a little more careful then. This is what happened in the Old Testament, but now God says it's done, it's all finished. And the reason for being so careful now is already done, the work is done. So now you can come in boldly and say, "God, here I am."

He said we can come boldly before the throne of grace:

> Let us therefore come boldly unto the throne of grace, that we may obtain mercy, and find grace to help in time of need (Hebrews 4:16).

The holiest place is where God lives; that's the center, it's the heart of God, and the blood opened the way so that we can have boldness to come right into where God is. You don't have to walk carefully now.

You can come skipping and jumping and leaping. And you don't have to come with silence. There could be no speaking at all in that holiest place when the priest was there; the blood had to do the speaking.

The Bible says it was the blood that carried the message, so in the Old Testament there could be no sound. But now He says we can come and shout aloud. When John had a chance to visit heaven and saw this beautiful throne of God, he said he saw people before the throne who were shouting with a loud voice that sounded like a great waterfall because they were praising God for what He had done. All of this carefulness has been removed to where we can come into God's presence in Jesus' name. Don't you love Him? So we have boldness to enter.

> By a new and living way, which he hath consecrated for us, through the veil, that is to say, his flesh; And having an high priest over the house of God; Let us draw near with a true heart in full assurance of faith, having our hearts sprinkled from an evil conscience, and our bodies washed with pure water. Let us hold fast the profession of our faith without wavering (for he is faithful that promised); And let us consider one another to provoke unto love and to good works: Not forsaking the assembling of ourselves together, as the manner of some is; but exhorting one another: and so much the more, as ye see the day approaching (Hebrews 10:20-25).

So He tells us we can come. God has not only invited us to come, but He's prepared a spot for us. He says, "I have a very honored spot for you, and you can come now as kings and priests unto God."

> And they sung a new song, saying, Thou art worthy to take the book, and to open the seals thereof: for thou wast slain, and hast redeemed us to God by thy blood out of every kindred, and tongue, and people, and nation; And hast made us unto our God kings and priests: and we shall reign on the earth (Revelation 5:9-10).

In this passage, John tells us what he had a chance to see. He says we are made kings and priests, a real special place that God Himself honors. Then I want you to notice the results of living in His presence. David discovered this because in His presence is where the fellowship is, you see.

> Thou wilt shew me the path of life: in thy presence is fullness of joy; at thy right hand there are pleasures for evermore (Psalm 16:11).

This is what happens in the presence of God. It's joy, it's not a drag. When God beams down His life, there's joy—there's a real bounce that comes with His presence. There's satisfaction, there's protection in His presence.

> Blessed is the man whom thou choosest, and causest to approach unto thee, that he may dwell in thy courts: we shall be satisfied with the goodness of thy house, even of thy holy temple (Psalm 65:4).

> Oh how great is thy goodness, which thou hast laid up for them that fear thee; which thou hast wrought for them that trust in thee before the sons of men! Thou shalt hide them in the secret of thy presence from the pride of man: thou shalt keep them secretly in a pavilion from the strife of tongues (Psalm 31:19-20).

Regardless of what people may say against you, there is a hiding place, a place by Him. There's a little truth here in that word "secret." When He says the "secret" of His presence, He is pointing to the fact that there is a secret force or power that is emanating from His beautiful presence. It's something that people cannot see from the outside; it's an invisible force.

The enemy may wonder how God can protect those people—they look like they're all exposed there. He comes roaring up to hit you and he finds that there's a force field around you. That's the secret of His presence. People who are close to God are more interested in what God has to say than what people have to say.

> But if we walk in the light, as he is in the light, we have fellowship one with another, and the blood of Jesus Christ his Son cleanseth us from all sin (1 John 1:7).

John speaks of the fellowship we have with Him. Communion with God is something more than communication. Communication may be the passing of information, getting the thoughts straight, getting the words straight. But communion is when your heart speaks and there's a heart fellowship—an oneness of spirit with God. This is what communion is. Have you noticed this with people, that sometimes you can have heart communion with them and you haven't said anything? There's just a drawing toward them, a feeling that he's my brother or she's my sister in the Lord. This comes because God has let us come into His presence.

I'm going to try to share something the Lord made so real to me. I wept before God when I asked the Lord to make this as real to me as it was that night when He spoke it first to my heart. And God did make Himself so very real to me there. He is our High Priest.

There are so many beautiful verses here that I would like to encourage you to look up in your own Bible and read. Ask God to show you their meaning. We read these words:

> And they truly were many priests, because they were not suffered to continue by reason of death: But this man, because he continueth ever, hath an unchangeable priesthood. Wherefore he is able also to save them to the uttermost that come unto God by him, seeing he ever liveth to make intercession for them. For such an high priest became us, who is holy, harmless, undefiled, separate from sinners, and made higher

than the heavens; Who needeth not daily, as those high priests, to offer up sacrifice, first for his own sins, and then for the people's: for this he did once, when he offered up himself. For the law maketh men high priests which have infirmity; but the word of the oath, which was since the law, maketh the Son, who is consecrated for evermore (Hebrews 7:23-28).

Here is the main point—Our High Priest sat down in the place of highest honor in heaven, at God's right hand. There He ministers in the sacred tent, the true place of worship that was built by the Lord and not by human hands. In verse five He says, "They serve in a place of worship that is only a copy, a shadow of the real one in heaven." But Jesus is up there in the tabernacle that God pitched, making intercession for us. So what God has asked us to do when we come into His presence is to come like those priests did and to minister to God.

Now these priests as they ministered took their incense and burned it, which wafted up into that altar of incense as a sweet savor unto God. God said, "I am pleased, I am satisfied. I enjoy this sweet savor of this offering."

They ministered unto the Lord. It was a daily routine. Their daily routine actually became a priestly service. And our daily routine, the job that we are on, becomes priestly service. If you are a lady doing the tasks around the house or a man working in the yard, if you have a job, that daily routine becomes priestly service because a priest is performing it. Did you know you were a priest now?

And whatsoever ye do in word or deed, do all in the name of the Lord Jesus, giving thanks to God and the Father by him (Colossians 3:17).

Do it for God's glory. Now this is called ministering to the Lord. God is pleased with it. When you sit in His presence and you just draw from Him and you love Him, you're ministering to Jesus, you're serving Him.

The biggest lie that the enemy would like for us to believe is that feverish activity is serving the Lord or ministering to the Lord. That's not serving God. You may be getting a few things done and you may not be, but you're all tied up in knots trying to do God's work. God's work is to make you calm, and you're undoing God's work if you're all tied up in knots trying to please Him or minister to Him. If you want to minister to Him or just love Him, then do your job with a song in your heart—then you're ministering unto the Lord. This is what God has asked us to do. By the blood we can minister as unto Him. When we minister to Him, then we minister to others. We minister through prayer, through intercession, and by activating God's vast network of resources while considering ourselves as priests doing His work.

> Ye also, as lively stones, are built up a spiritual house, an holy priesthood, to offer up spiritual sacrifices, acceptable to God by Jesus Christ. Wherefore also it is contained in the scripture, Behold, I lay in Sion a chief corner stone, elect, precious: and he that believeth on him shall not be confounded. Unto you therefore which believe he is precious: but unto them which be disobedient, the stone which the builders disallowed, the same is made the head of the corner, And a stone of stumbling, and a rock of offence, even to them which stumble at the word, being disobedient: whereunto also they were appointed. But ye are a chosen generation, a royal priesthood, an holy nation, a peculiar people; that ye should shew forth the praises of him who hath called you out of darkness into his marvelous light (1 Peter 2:5-9).

You are a kingdom of priests, God's holy nation, and His very own possession so that you can show others the goodness of God. He called you out of the darkness into His wonderful light for this purpose.

You're a royal priesthood; you can come right into God's presence and minister to Him and then minister to others. We minister to others through prayer, and through prayer we activate the resources of heaven.

God gave me a vision of the Christian in prayer, and I watched as this Christian prayed. He pushed the buttons that would activate God's hand that would send whatever agency was necessary to get the job done. At God's command were hosts of angels that could come down and do it. There were people who didn't even know God—unbelievers—and God would needle in and tell them to get going and help that person. There were other believers, and God could say that person needs a five-dollar bill, give it to him. God has put it in some of your hearts to minister to people. There's a person who needs a little bit of help over there. She just needs a word of comfort, and you go do it. See, God sends the people to do it.

Then there's the power of the Holy Spirit and the ministry of the Spirit through His gifts. Then God has an agency that readjusts the circumstances. Not always do circumstances change; God often will change the person and leave the circumstances the same, but God can even readjust circumstances. Then in that vision God let me see Him calling His forces of nature, His creation, to getting a swarm of bees to get out and do the job for Him. Bees can hasten people along, but they can do some other things.

I'll never forget when my wife and I were in Washington, and a bunch of aphids came in overnight and landed in a big apple orchard. The man who owned the orchard had only been a Christian about three months, but he had been told that God was real, and so he figured if God was real He knew how to take care of things. So he went to fellowship meeting and told them to have a word of prayer with him so God would be reminded that there was a need over there. When he came home in the middle of the afternoon, he heard a strange humming sound.

And when God listened to that prayer He said, "What would be the best method to get rid of all of those aphids? I could take a big wind and bring my heavenly vacuum cleaner and suck all those leaves clean. But

I have a bunch of hungry bees over here that need the food; I'll do two things at once."

So He gathered millions of hungry bees and dumped them into this man's orchard, and they had the biggest feast they ever had in their life. They picked every aphid off of those leaves. There wasn't one left. But God only sent enough bees to clean out that one field. Everybody else's orchards were still filled with aphids. God has access to whatever agency—He knows how to fix things. If it's the weather, God can change that. God isn't bound in following only one little narrow channel in answering prayer like we think—He is in control of the whole universe.

So in prayer we can minister and carry the blessing of God to others and share with them of His life and His love. That's why we read that verse in 1 John 1 that our job is to declare unto others about this wonderful fellowship. And surely the thing that we really need in our life is to have fellowship with our heavenly Father.

It's the search, the hunger of men and women down through the ages just to be able to get close to God again. And the work that we're doing, the work that you're doing in helping people, the main aim of that work is so that they can have fellowship with Jesus. Isn't that right? Fellowship was made possible because of the blood. Without the blood there could be no fellowship at all.

In conclusion, Jesus unlocked the grave with His blood. Hebrews 13:20 says that by His own blood He came forth from the grave:

> Now the God of peace, that brought again from the dead our
> Lord Jesus, that great shepherd of the sheep, through the blood
> of the everlasting covenant (Hebrews 13:20).

He unlocked heaven. With His blood He entered into the presence of God. With His blood He unlocked God's heart.

> Having therefore, brethren, boldness to enter into the holiest
> by the blood of Jesus (Hebrews 10:19).

And they truly were many priests, because they were not suffered to continue by reason of death (Hebrews 7:23).

Now of the things which we have spoken this is the sum: We have such an high priest, who is set on the right hand of the throne of the Majesty in the heavens (Hebrews 8:1).

Having boldness to enter now by the blood of Jesus opened God's heart. This is the summary of the whole thing. We have a Priest now who is seated at the right hand of God. In the Old Testament, the priest could not sit down. He had to stand the entire time he was working, signifying the fact that the work was never quite completed; it was a continuing thing year after year, year after year. But now it says Jesus finished the work, and He sat down. He "got it done!"

So we have a High Priest today seated at the right hand of God. His sacrifice has been accepted, His work has been completed. It's done. He looked at it, and He said it's working, there it is, the blood is there, it's incorruptible; it will just keep right on working. And Jesus looked at it and said, "Father, how does it look?" God said, "I accept it, it's done, it's done, here have a seat." He sat down; Jesus isn't struggling. He's not worrying. God isn't worrying about it. God knows it's good. It's been good for nearly two thousand years, and it's not going to stop. Jesus is resting in assurance that it's done. It's made forever, no more need to be done. And so He can't figure out why in the world we're so worried about it. God isn't worried about it, He said it's working. Jesus isn't worried about it; He sat down and said it's done. Let's quit worrying about it and sweating about it. The blood has never lost its power.

He said there remains a rest for the people of God. What joy we possess when we catch a little bit of the message that Jesus brought—that the blood will never be destroyed, that it's incorruptible, that it will keep on doing the work, that it's all powerful, it will just keep on moving, it will never, never, never cease. When we can catch that glimpse, then we can enter into that same rest.

For he that is entered into his rest, he also hath ceased from
his own works, as God did from his (Hebrews 4:10).

I got so excited when the Lord revealed this to me that I could hardly
stand it. And I would just love to have rubbed a little bit off on you. So
He wants us to quit struggling. Thank God for the blood that's still effective and our High Priest, who is still there sitting down at the right hand
of the Father.

To us, what is that river? What is the visible, tangible channel, what
is the pipeline that draws this river, that washes away the barrier, that
washes away the records, that washes away the sin, that brings the life,
that destroys the distance that's between? What is the tangible thing
that we can lay hold of? It's the name of Jesus. This is the reason why
I encourage people, and I'll never get away from this because I see it's
the most effective way of drawing what God has provided that there can
possibly be, so I ask people to call the name of Jesus, for as we call that
name, that name becomes a mighty pipeline, and God pours through it
of this life to us. They that call on the name of the Lord, that name Jesus,
shall be saved. That river flows, washes away the sin, and washes away
the barrier.

So all of these benefits of the blood of Jesus that come to us come
by the name of Jesus. Lift your heart and breathe from deep within the
name of Jesus, and let Him do whatever is necessary in your life as that
river flows from God's heart right through you. Jesus, Jesus, Jesus...

Chapter Eight

THERE IS LIFE in the BLOOD of JESUS

THE MESSAGE GOD wove into His Word on the power of Jesus' blood is like a brilliant diamond sparkling in the sun with multicolored, multi-faceted truths. As the light of heaven shines upon this revelation of the blood of Jesus, we are overwhelmed by the beauty and the completeness of God's plan of restoration. In this study we have seen a river of life from God's heart burst forth at Calvary, sweep away the separating barriers, destroy the records of sin, transport its Divine Life, and carry us in its current to a place close to God's heart. Another facet of beauty we will view in this lesson is the life of this blood and what it means to us.

I will try to explain a vision God allowed me to see of the beauty of the tabernacle of God in heaven. It was constructed and planned before the foundation of the earth, yet the structure before me was cold, powerless, and lifeless as it was not in operation, awaiting the application of life, which is in the blood. God let me see Jesus take His own blood and enter into the tabernacle.

God said to me, "I want you to see the power of this blood—the life is in the blood." So Jesus went into the tabernacle and sprinkled the articles of furniture with His own blood.

Suddenly, all the wheels of God's great plan began to turn. Sins from Adam to sins of the present and even to sins of the future were atoned for by the blood. All of those things that had been waiting—a great big backlog of sin was there waiting to be taken away, but God said those Old Testament sacrifices could never take away sins being brought there. Year after year they were waiting until the machine in heaven would start to move—and the only way it could possibly run was by the blood of Jesus. God let me see the power of the blood of Jesus in God's great plan as it worked, reaching out across the ages that still had not happened, clear to the end of time, and withdrawing every sin, every iniquity, and destroying, their power.

You realize there are many people who are still carrying sin. They haven't availed themselves of what God has done. That's why Paul said they are suffering the motions of sins that are already taken care of. John said that Christ has become the propitiation for our sins, and not for ours only, but for the sins of the whole world. Paul said in Hebrews ten that this Man Jesus made one sacrifice for sin forever. It's done, it's working, and He sat down at the right hand of God. The sacrifice of the blood takes care of the past, present and future.

Hebrews 9 in the Living Bible says, "Now in that first agreement between God and his people there were rules for worship and there was a sacred tent down here on earth. Inside this place of worship there were two rooms. The first one contained the golden candlestick and a table with special loaves of holy bread upon it; this part was called the Holy Place. Then there was a curtain and behind the curtain was a room called the Holy of Holies. In that room there were a golden incense altar and the golden chest called the ark of the covenant, completely covered on all sides with pure gold. Inside the ark were the tablets of stone with the Ten Commandments written on them, and a golden jar with some manna in it, and Aaron's wooden cane that budded. Above the golden chest were statues of angels called the cherubim—the guardians of God's glory—with their wings stretched out over the ark's golden cover called the mercy seat. But enough of such detail. Well, when all was ready the priests went in and out of the first room whenever they wanted to, doing their work. But only the high priest went into the inner room and then only once a year, all alone, and always with blood, which he sprinkled on the mercy seat as an offering to God to cover his own mistakes and sins, and the mistakes and sins of all the people. And the Holy Spirit uses all this to point out to us that under the old system the common people could not go into the Holy of Holies as long as the outer room and the entire system it represents were still in use" (Hebrews 9:1-8 TLB).

Now this has an important lesson for us today for, under the old system, gifts and sacrifices were offered but failed to cleanse the hearts of the people who brought them. The old system dealt only with certain rituals—what foods to eat, what to drink, rules for washing their bodies, rules about this and rules about that. The people had to keep these rules to tide them over until Christ came with God's new and better way. He came as High Priest of this better system, which we now have. He went into the greater, perfect tabernacle in heaven not made by men or being a part of this world. It only took one time. Jesus entered the Holy of Holies with blood and sprinkled it on the mercy seat—but it was not the blood of goats and calves. No, He took His own blood, and with that precious, most valuable blood, He made sure of our eternal salvation.

"If under the old system the blood of bulls and goats and the ashes of young cows would cleanse men's bodies from sin, just think how much more surely the blood of Christ will transform our lives and hearts. His sacrifice frees us from the worry of having to obey the old rules and makes us want to serve the

Living God. His sacrifice frees us from the worry of having to obey the old rules and makes us want to serve the Living God. For by the help of the Eternal Holy Spirit, Christ willingly gave Himself to God to die for our sins. He being perfect without a single sin or fault came with this new agreement so that all who are invited may come and have forever all of the wonders that God has promised them. Christ died to rescue them from the penalty of sins that they had committed while still under that old system." (Hebrews 9:13-15)

All of these tabernacle furnishings were so important because God was showing us His attitude—His plan for helping man through this life:

- The candlestick to give us light—God's light
- The table of shewbread that spoke of communion, that He had made it possible for man to have communion with Him
- The brazen altar, which made possible a substitute for sin to be taken
- The laver of cleansing set in the center of the pathway to the Holy place, not off to the side, so that there would be that constant cleansing as we walked through life
- The beautiful altar of incense, where He said, "Your prayers please God when you come to Him, and they ascend up as sweet incense in the nostrils of God."
- The throne room, where the heavenly beings stand with their wings outstretched over this altar, this throne of God
- The mercy seat—God said to Moses in Exodus 25 that there is only one place in the whole universe that He would meet with man, and that's the spot where you come and you identify and you're accepted, because all of your

sins are underneath the mercy seat, and God can't see them.

Each of these furnishings represents the steps that Jesus took to bring us into fellowship with God our Father, Jesus our Brother, and the Holy Spirit our Teacher. God is now accessible to people.

Now all of this was already made in a pattern in heaven, but it wasn't working for those of us on earth. It meant nothing yet—it had to have some life to work. This was a tedious thing for Israel to have to go through every year. Each step was so detailed, so perfect, because Christ was the one who followed those details. I've heard people teaching on the tabernacle say in our worship every detail has to be just exactly perfect. You're not Christ—you're not preparing yourself for the sacrifice. The work is already done, and so it isn't a matter now of our having to go through this process to get to God. Christ sat down and made one sacrifice forever. He finished the work and the wheels were set in motion in heaven, and they're still turning. Christ provided the perfect sacrifice. He sat down at the right hand of God forever. He said it is working.

Once a year the priest went into the Holiest of Holies to sprinkle blood on the mercy seat. Blood was so important to God. Verse eight was the verse that God gave to me so clearly that night:

The Holy Ghost signifying that the way into the holiest of all was not yet made manifest where as yet the first tabernacle was still standing (Hebrews 9:8).

I see something here that God really spoke to my heart about. People who are putting their faith in what they are able to do by ceremony and by their own production cease to avail themselves of what Jesus has done because they're still struggling. There's still that work, that frustration, a worry over doing something right in order to get to God. Paul mentioned this in Galatians 5:4 where he said, "Christ has become of no effect unto you." In essence, Paul is saying that God has the job all done, but the people were trying to do it over again. We can't justify ourselves by what we're able to produce.

We should say, "God, I'll come your way."

But sometimes people say, "No thanks, God, I'd rather do it myself."

I wish people wouldn't try to weaken what God says because they're afraid they won't go to heaven for sure—a fear otherwise known as eternal security. God didn't say for us to shun eternal security. He says to claim eternal security because it's there. He said He obtained eternal redemption for us. He did tell us that He wasn't going to force it on us, and if we took a bite and didn't like it He wasn't going to tie us there. He doesn't want anybody in heaven who doesn't want to go there. God does not do things halfway. His plan was for a complete and wonderful salvation that would sweep us right on into heaven because He doesn't do things halfway. Whatever He did, the Word tells us, "He saw it and it was good," and He did a good job. So if we would quit looking for holes that we could fall out of and look at what God has prepared and what He's doing, we would be a lot better off.

> For the life of the flesh is in the blood: and I have given it to you upon the altar to make an atonement for your souls: for it is the blood that maketh an atonement for the soul. For it is the life of all flesh; the blood of it is for the life thereof: therefore I said unto the children of Israel, Ye shall eat the blood of no manner of flesh: for the life of all flesh is the blood thereof: whosoever eateth it shall be cut off (Leviticus 17:11,14).

God is saying, "I have given you the blood so you can make atonement for your sins. The life of every creature is in the blood. That is why I have told the people of Israel never to eat or drink it, for the life of any bird or animal is in the blood. So whoever eats or drinks blood must be cut off."

These facets of truth that I want to show you point to the power that the life of Jesus brings when applied. The tabernacle in heaven and all of God's great plan didn't go into effect until the blood was applied, and then it started to move. The same goes for the atonement.

Because His blood is living and contains all the power of the entire Godhead, all the power of creation is in that blood. God told Moses, "I want you to take that blood because the life is in it. It's going to be able to make atonement—it's going to be able to speak."

The animal that was slain represented life, and in tabernacle worship the priest could not say one word while he was in that holy place. There was to be no sound in that place. They couldn't even make any sound in that place when they were building it. That was a holy place. When the priest entered there, God wanted to let the people know that He listened to another kind of voice. When he came in with that blood, the blood spoke!

If you remember, God let Paul have a glimpse of heaven, and he saw the Father, Jesus, and an innumerable company of angels. What's amazing is that Paul happened to look over, and he said, "There's the blood, and look! It's still speaking. It's speaking to God."

The blood is eternal—it will never lose its power. And so when Christ went in, His blood carried a message to God, and when He applied it to the mercy seat, to the tabernacle, all at once God's ears picked up the message. The blood was speaking and it was saying, "They're forgiven. Their sins are destroyed. The records are gone. That blood has atoned."

God's planning is so unique and beautiful. Every little old part of God's plan is so well synchronized with everything else—and to think that God would even make a word that would say what He wanted to say when there are so many thousands and thousands of words. How could He put one together that was there? But He did. The word atonement in the Hebrew language is pronounced *Kawhfer*. And this word has nine definitions in that Hebrew dictionary. God included in that word atonement everything that needed to be said. The blood was speaking, and here are the things that He covered in that:

1. That word atonement means first of all *to cover.* God can't see the sin. When you said, "Jesus I give you my life," God took a blanket and covered your life, and you were covered with His robe of righteousness. And God looks down at you and says, "Perfect, perfect."

   And therefore it was imputed to him for righteousness. [23]Now it was not written for his sake alone, that it was imputed to him; [24]But for us also, to whom it shall be imputed, if we believe on him that raised up Jesus our Lord from the dead (Romans 4:22-24).

And so God looks at people—some real good people, some medium good people, some medium bad people, and some that are real bad, but they're all putting their faith in Jesus, and He says, "They're all level."

   Not that we are sufficient of ourselves to think any thing as of ourselves; but our sufficiency is of God (2 Corinthians 3:5).

2. The second meaning of the word atonement is *to expiate, to remove the old thing that was in the way, to cancel the debt.* The word in the Greek for atonement is propitiation. So it means Jesus has become the covering for our sin.

   And he is the propitiation for our sins: and not for ours only, but also for the sins of the whole world (1 John 2:2).

That's what atonement is doing. When the enemy comes up and says, "Hey, God, that person's really in debt. I know they did this." God says, "There's a voice coming from this blood that says the debt is all taken care of." And it has to keep speaking because we keep getting ourselves into trouble, and the blood just has to keep on talking. It's a message that just keeps on going up before God.

3. The third meaning of the word atonement is *to appease the wrath or remove the cause of wrath so God is not angry anymore.* We're not enemies anymore.

   But if we walk in the light, as he is in the light, we have fellowship one with another, and the blood of Jesus Christ his Son cleanseth us from all sin (1John 1:7).

4. A fourth meaning of atonement is *to disannul.* This means *to render the charges void, to obliterate the pronounced sentence, to remove whatever is there.* The pronounced sentence of death is abolished. The Bible says that the soul that sins shall die, but the atonement says, "I'm disannulling this thing that was against you, I'm destroying it." Leaving this body isn't death. Eternal death is that sentence of death that separates you from God.

   But is now made manifest by the appearing of our Saviour Jesus Christ, who hath abolished death, and hath brought life and immortality to light through the gospel (2 Timothy 1:10).

5. A fifth definition of the word atonement is *forgiveness, restored to the original place in God's heart the spot that He had when He created Adam and Eve.*

6. Another meaning is *to obtain mercy.*

7. The best definition for atonement is *kindness with sympathy.* People can be kind and still not feel. But when mercy is shown, it is kindness with sympathy.

8. Atonement purges. This atonement has a purging, cleansing influence.

   How much more shall the blood of Christ, who through the eternal Spirit offered himself without spot to God, purge your conscience from dead works to serve the living God (Hebrews 9:14)?

9. The last definition for atonement is to *reconcile and to make peace.*

This leads us to the third great work accomplished through the life in the blood of Jesus. Let's review:

1. The blood made the tabernacle come alive.
2. The blood of Jesus made the atonement go to work because of the life of Jesus.
3. The blood makes God's Word come alive.

Because of the blood, the Bible can be more to you than just a book. It can be a living, pulsating Word from God Himself. It is alive, and its life is activated by the Blood.

> For the word of God is quick, and powerful, and sharper than any two-edged sword, piercing even to the dividing asunder of soul and spirit, and of the joints and marrow, and is a discerner of the thoughts and intents of the heart (Hebrews 4:12).

God said that the Word is quick and that word quick means *alive.* So the Word of God, because of the blood of Jesus, becomes a living, pulsating thing—different from all other books. The Bible has life circulating through every page and every verse. It's alive! No wonder it gets a hold of you and will do things for you that no other book can do.

> It is the spirit that quickeneth; the flesh profiteth nothing: the words that I speak unto you, they are spirit, and they are life (John 6:63).

Being born again, not of corruptible seed, but of incorruptible, by the word of God, which liveth and abideth for ever. For all flesh is as grass, and all the glory of man as the flower of grass. The grass withereth, and the flower thereof falleth away: But the word of the Lord endureth for ever. And this is the word which by the gospel is preached unto you (1 Peter 1:23-25).

That Word is the Good News that was preached to us. Peter tells us we have not been redeemed by corruptible things such as silver or gold but with the precious blood of Christ. Every drop of Jesus' blood that fell to the ground did not fall there and become part of the ground and lost. The Word tells us that His blood was incorruptible. God kept every bit. The picture that He gave in the tabernacle was in the place where the blood of the sacrificial lamb was slain; there had to be a little trough.

The reason why He had to have it so exact was that God said, "I'm not going to let any of this fall to the ground. It is preserved forever—it's incorruptible." That is why the Bible says, "Forever, Oh Lord, Your Word is settled and will never be destroyed." Infidels have tried to destroy it, people have burned up the paper and the print, but the Word just keeps going on. It's the Living Word.

What are some of the blessings of the Word when it is alive?

- It comforts
- It inspires
- It brings peace
- It is actually a companion
- It rebukes us
- It speaks to us
- It convicts us
- It makes us feel like we are standing on solid ground
- It provides assurance
- It feeds us
- It directs us and says, "That's the way to go."

- If you can't see where you're going, it's a light
- It reveals Jesus
- The Word of God holds Him up in all of His beauty for us to see
- The Word corrects us and shows us where we have gone astray

Abundant victorious living is within the reach of all because of what has been accomplished by the blood of Jesus. Now we can have boldness to enter into the holiest, most sacred room by the blood of Jesus. The past, present, and future are all included in the atonement.

So even the very word that God chose—atonement—would say everything God wanted it to say. The atonement—the blood—is still speaking. When Paul had a chance to visit heaven, he saw the spirits of just men made perfect, and he said, "There's the blood, and it's still speaking."

One of the things that troubles many people is the past. Then there's another bunch of people who are afraid of what hasn't happened yet. But all God gives us is strength for today, so we get into trouble when we start pulling from yesterday's problems. We get into trouble when we pull on tomorrow's, because we may never get there.

> For Christ is not entered into the holy places made with hands, which are the figures of the true; but into heaven itself, now to appear in the presence of God for us: ^{25}Nor yet that he should offer himself often, as the high priest entereth into the holy place every year with blood of others; ^{26}For then must he often have suffered since the foundation of the world: but now once in the end of the world hath he appeared to put away sin by the sacrifice of himself. ^{27}And as it is appointed unto men once to die, but after this the judgment: ^{28}So Christ was once offered to bear the sins of many; and unto them that look for him shall he appear the second time without sin unto salvation (Hebrews 9:24-28).

Everybody knows that death is certain. If you believe that death is sure, you can also believe that He will appear. So the blood of Jesus Christ tells us that because of the power of His blood He's going to come back for us who are without sin. Without the living blood, God's great plan of the sanctuary would be like a highly developed engine without a force to activate it. A lot of people don't realize the present work of Jesus. The sacrifice flows as far as His light. This ties in with 1 John 1:7:

> But if we walk in the light, as he is in the light, we have fellowship one with another, and the blood of Jesus Christ his Son cleanseth us from all sin (1 John 1:7).

What happens if you decide to quit and pursue sin anyway? You may say, "God, I know that you hate this thing, but I'm going to break fellowship for a little while. I'm going to go out and do this thing that you hate." God says the sacrifice doesn't flow that far. The one who does that has to come back and say, "Jesus, let your blood flow again."

It's a dangerous business for people to take themselves out of God's care. The Lord knows the way of the righteous, and everything that happens in that sphere is beautiful fellowship. But the way of the unrighteous, those who get out from under this fellowship and are proving they are unrighteous by wanting to willfully disobey God, those people are in an area where they will perish. The enemy can do a lot of things to us when we are out of fellowship with God.

Many are called, but few people have chosen to accept the call. God has chosen them all. He wasn't willing that any should perish but all should come to repentance. God will help each of us and urge us to get to that door of decision, but when we stand at that door, He said we have to choose.

Chapter Nine

THE COMMUNION of the BLOOD

W E SEE MANY bright rays of truth beamed to us from God's
message in blood:

- His wrath is turned away
- The records of sin are gone
- Distance between us has been removed
- Guilt is gone
- His life flows through these mortal bodies

In this chapter we will take a look at possibly the highest purpose God
had in mind through the flow of this crimson stream—restoration to a
place of communion, where there is an oneness of spirit between God
and man.

And folks, this is what communion really is. Communion is not just
the act of the taking of symbols of His death (the bread and wine or
grape juice), but it is an oneness of spirit between us and God.
In the Old Testament the communion, as we know it, was called the
Passover.

And the blood shall be to you for a token upon the houses where ye are: and when I see the blood, I will pass over you, and the plague shall not be upon you to destroy you, when I smite the land of Egypt. And this day shall be unto you for a memorial; and ye shall keep it a feast to the LORD throughout your generations; ye shall keep it a feast by an ordinance for ever. And ye shall observe this thing for an ordinance to thee and to thy sons for ever (Exodus 12:13,14,24).

That word instruction means *a law,* and in this particular case, because God gave it, it became a divine law. God gave this as a law because there is no life in the individual without partaking of Jesus. This Passover was a symbol of the Lamb that would come.

These families partook of the lamb:

- They used the blood for protection
- They used the body for food
- They used the body for their physical health

And so the Word tells us in speaking about this that in the body of Jesus, the reason many people are so weak and sick is because they haven't discerned the Lord's body. Someone can accept the forgiveness which comes from the blood yet not discern the body of Christ. And when we partake of His life, we are not only taking of the blood but also of the virtues of His body.

Now we may think the human body isn't worth very much, but to God it is of tremendous value because in the atonement and in His plan before He ever started the world, He made provision for the health of the body.

Surely he hath borne our griefs, and carried our sorrows: yet we did esteem him stricken, smitten of God, and afflicted. [5]But he was wounded for our transgressions, he was bruised for our iniquities: the chastisement of our peace was upon him; and with his stripes we are healed (Isaiah 53:4,5).

Wherefore whosoever shall eat this bread, and drink this cup of the Lord, unworthily, shall be guilty of the body and blood of the Lord. But let a man examine himself, and so let him eat of that bread, and drink of that cup. For he that eateth and drinketh unworthily, eateth and drinketh damnation to himself, not discerning the Lord's body (1 Corinthians 11:27-29).

But when we are in God's presence and we take the full focus of what He intended through communion, we receive:

- Emotional healing
- Physical healing
- Spiritual healing

That's why Paul in his prayer states:

And the very God of peace sanctify you wholly; and I pray God your whole spirit and soul and body be preserved blameless unto the coming of our Lord Jesus Christ (1 Thessalonians 5:23).

Well, God made room for preservation, and any time we get off on just one little binge or another we're missing God completely. His life provides this. It doesn't mean that if a person is sick that he is not partaking of His life. God has timing and purposes, and He's looking at it from a different angle than we are. His mercies are new every day. Even physical health isn't always what people assume it to be, but when you come into God's presence and He shares His life with you, you feel that glow and that flow.

There are people who have the anointing of the Spirit just as strong who may not receive the physical evidence of healing. But they have evidences that His life is there. You can go your way happy, rejoicing even though you may have some symptoms of these things that are there. If God has touched you, you can thank God.

Many of the people whom I have seen healed in just recent weeks have been healed without their even asking God for it, and without my knowing anything about it. But God certainly knew, and when His life came, it took care of it. I think of one lady in particular. She came into the room almost dead and left almost dead. She came in sad dead and walked out happy dead. But three days later the symptoms of health came to her life.

This is the beautiful provision that God made. He said, "I want it to be a law forever." This was the Passover. And so the children of Israel every year had to keep that Passover.

When Jesus came, He said, "I'm taking away the old covenant, and I'm bringing in the new at the completion of my sacrifice."

Now the Passover isn't done away with, but the real Passover Lamb has come. You're able to partake of the real Lamb and the real blood. It won't be a matter of postponing or the symbol of the real, you will be partaking of the real. So when we think of the power of the blood, the breaking down of the barrier, the reconciliation, the removing of the records, the removing of the pollution of sin—all of these things were brought to man in order to bring about communion. God wanted to prepare man so He could have communion with him once again.

The only guarantee of acceptance before God is the blood. That's why it says the blood shall be to you a token and, when I look at it, when I see that the blood is there, you are accepted before Me. That blood is the mark. The blood is the only source of divine life.

> Then Jesus said unto them, Verily, verily, I say unto you, Except ye eat the flesh of the Son of man, and drink his blood, ye have no life in you. Whoso eateth my flesh, and drinketh my blood, hath eternal life; and I will raise him up at the last day. For

my flesh is meat indeed, and my blood is drink indeed. He that eateth my flesh, and drinketh my blood, dwelleth in me, and I in him. As the living Father hath sent me, and I live by the Father: so he that eateth me, even he shall live by me (John 6:53-57).

There's that fellowship, that communion now. We partake of Him and we live by Him—we have life! But He said if we don't partake of His flesh and blood, we have no life. He said if we do partake of His life, we'll abide together and we'll have fellowship with Him, and we have the promise of the resurrection from the dead or of the rapture (if we're still here and alive at the time), whichever case may be.

For this cause many are weak and sickly among you, and many sleep (1 Corinthians 11:30).

The verses leading up to this talk about communion and the need to partake of Him—they also speak about eating and drinking unworthily.

Wherefore whosoever shall eat this bread, and drink this cup of the Lord, unworthily, shall be guilty of the body and blood of the Lord. But let a man examine himself, and so let him eat of that bread, and drink of that cup. For he that eateth and drinketh unworthily, eateth and drinketh damnation to himself, not discerning the Lord's body. For this cause many are weak and sickly among you, and many sleep. For if we would judge ourselves, we should not be judged. But when we are judged, we are chastened of the Lord, that we should not be condemned with the world (1 Corinthians 11:27-32).

Sadly, these verses have been delivered as a threat to people for years and years. One popular interpretation is that drinking unworthily means that you took communion while you had something in your heart that wasn't right. But that interpretation is wrong. What he's telling you here when he says if you eat and drink without faith in the blood, you are drinking unworthily. If your faith is in what you have accomplished, then you are drinking unworthily. If you can sit there and say, "I've done this and this and this, and everything is okay, so I'm worthy," you are not availing yourself of true communion.

Paul used the term here that he has never expanded into a doctrine. Let's look at what Jesus said:

> For God sent not his Son into the world to condemn the world; but that the world through him might be saved. He that believeth on him is not condemned: but he that believeth not is condemned already, because he hath not believed in the name of the only begotten Son of God (John 3:17-18).

If we are depending on what we can do (the right prayer or an especially good deed), we are just eating and drinking in that state of condemnation because we haven't accepted Him, His life, and His body as all we need for salvation and fellowship. Because of this teaching, I think that many times God has not judged Christians because they partake of communion improperly. God knows the reasons why we respond as we do, and He looks at the heart. In many cases, God doesn't write it down because He sees the pressures that are causing our improper participation in communion, and He knows that it is not the true feeling of our heart. Oftentimes we do what we feel is expected in pleasing God, and God sees this. Sadly, it does rob us then of the ability to let our faith take hold of what Jesus has done. These are some of the thoughts or concerns that folks may have when they approach the communion table:

- I can't take communion today because there was that little thought that passed into my mind that wasn't right
- I'm guilty of some sins of omission; I could have done some good that I didn't do

- We had a little altercation at our house, and I didn't speak as nicely as I should have
- Look at all of these reasons why I shouldn't partake of Jesus

If this is you, look out! Satan will never let you run out of reasons. So the Lord doesn't want us to look for those reasons why we can't participate but look for the reasons why we can participate because His blood is for you—His blood is for me!

The blood that was shed for us in communion now is taken and given to us. We can partake of it and let it become part of our life—the injection of divine life. When our faith is not in the blood, it has to be in something else, and usually the emphasis is on examining oneself to see whether there are some things in us that would keep us from God. There's really no mention of that at all. When he says, "Let a man examine himself and so let him eat," the writer is saying a person needs to examine himself to see whether he is putting his faith in that blood. God isn't looking for reasons to condemn people; He came that we might have life.

For the first 1,750 years of the Christian experience, they didn't teach that people should examine themselves. That didn't start until the last part of the nineteenth century. Somebody got the idea that they needed to start putting people into an examination. But it wasn't in any print, and it wasn't accepted in any of the writings of the people down through those years until the last part of the nineteenth century. Then, all of a sudden, people started saying, "You've got to struggle and climb to a place of almost perfection before you can even partake of the life in communion." It's as much as saying you need to be strong and perfect before you're even alive. Jesus said if you don't take it, you don't have any life.

If you want Jesus, you hold the key right in your hand when you hold that cup and put your faith in what He has done. And the Lord isn't making it just a psychological thing but a change of mind. He likes to see how communion pushes the switch and people's lives are turned around. The new birth comes, and it happens. Our real communion that we have with God when we accept Him is not necessarily the celebration that we have. We feed on Him, and He feeds on our fellowship as we are in His presence. Every day we are having beautiful communion, but those times when we have celebration we're celebrating what we're doing. We can't see the blood that God has sprinkled on our life, but God can. It's happening every day as we fellowship and commune with Him. We're feeding His heart and He's feeding ours—that's communion.

How often should we take communion? I would hate to have to wait seven days before I had communion. The Lord wants us to have it every day in our own homes, and if people want to celebrate every week with their church, that's wonderful. But that is just a symbol of what really happens. The Lord comes and celebrates with you. God isn't nearly as interested in the details as He is in getting people into communion with Him.

Let's look at this story about King Hezekiah:

> For there were many in the congregation that were not sancti-fied: therefore the Levites had the charge of the killing of the passovers for every one that was not clean, to sanctify them unto the LORD. For a multitude of the people, even many of Ephraim, and Manasseh, Issachar, and Zebulun, had not cleansed themselves, yet did they eat the passover otherwise than it was written. But Hezekiah prayed for them, saying, The good LORD pardon every one That prepareth his heart to seek God, the LORD God of his fathers, though he be not cleansed according to the purification of the sanctuary. And the LORD hearkened to Hezekiah, and healed the people (2 Chronicles 30:17-20).

This is a story of people who hadn't purified themselves after the purification of the temple. They hadn't examined themselves to see whether they had some bad feelings or other things, and here they were taking of the Passover, and they scared the priests half to death. And so the priests came to Hezekiah and said, "What are we going to do? Those people haven't followed the rules."

And Hezekiah said, "Well, let's find out what God thinks."

And God said, "I like it," and He forgave all of them.

This communion and forgiveness is placed in New Testament worship. The completed sacrifice of Jesus activated a new covenant so it fulfilled the law of Moses and began the law of Christ—the law of love, which is written on the heart.

> But now hath he obtained a more excellent ministry, by how much also he is the mediator of a better covenant, which was established upon better promises. For if that first covenant had been faultless, then should no place have been sought for the second. For finding fault with them, he saith, Behold, the days come, saith the Lord, when I will make a new covenant with the house of Israel and with the house of Judah: Not according to the covenant that I made with their fathers in the day when I took them by the hand to lead them out of the land of Egypt; because they continued not in my covenant, and I regarded them not, saith the Lord. For this is the covenant that I will make with the house of Israel after those days, saith the Lord; I will put my laws into their mind, and write them in their hearts: and I will be to them a God, and they shall be to me a people: And they shall not teach every man his neighbour, and every man his brother, saying, Know the Lord: for all shall know me, from the least to the greatest. For I will be merciful to their unrighteousness, and their sins and their iniquities will I remember no more. In that he saith, A new covenant, he hath made the first old. Now that which decayeth and waxeth old is ready to vanish away (Hebrews 8:6-13).

In this passage we see that Christ began the new covenant and wrote a new "law" on the fleshy tablets of the heart instead of the cold stones Moses carried. Jesus was ushering in a new covenant. The new covenant says, "I will be merciful to your unrighteousness, and I will not remember your sin."

He didn't say, "I'm going to spare you people who are righteous." No, he said, "I will be merciful to your unrighteousness and your sins, and your iniquities will I remember no more because here's the blood."

Friend, even though God made this revelation on the power of the blood of Jesus real to me that night when He gave me this message, the impact of this message didn't strike me right away. For several years I didn't move into this revelation even though I had it written out after the Lord gave it to me. Honestly, I had forgotten that I had it written down until I took out the notes and put them together for these chapters on the power of the blood of Jesus.

The beautiful truth is that there is no life without the blood. Let's look at the passage that talks about the time Jesus had communion with his disciples:

> And as they were eating, Jesus took bread, and blessed it, and brake it, and gave it to the disciples, and said, Take, eat; this is my body. And he took the cup, and gave thanks, and gave it to them, saying, Drink ye all of it; For this is my blood of the new testament, which is shed for many for the remission of sins. But I say unto you, I will not drink henceforth of this fruit of the vine, until that day when I drink it new with you in my Father's kingdom (Matthew 26:26-29).

I looked in the commentaries and read what the Greek and Hebrew scholars had to say about this particular communion in Matthew. They put this time that Jesus is speaking about into the kingdom reign, where Jesus said this is the last time and I will not do it until my Father's kingdom. But in looking at these notes that I scribbled out that God put in my heart,

Jesus said, "The completion of my sacrifice began the kingdom life." The Lord tied that thought in with Isaiah 55:3 and Isaiah 54:

> Incline your ear, and come unto me: hear, and your soul shall live; and I will make an everlasting covenant with you, even the sure mercies of David (Isaiah 55:3).

And so the kingdom life and promises belong to the people who are part of His kingdom. I read those notes and got so excited because I had written down in the new covenant the words of Jesus that John the Beloved documented:

> Behold, I stand at the door, and knock: if any man hear my voice, and open the door, I will come in to him, and will sup with him, and he with me (Revelation 3:20).

It is exciting because this isn't something that's way off in the future, but it's right now. Jesus is there "supping," or fellowshipping, with us right now. God was concerned about this because, as I had written down that day of the vision, if this were something of a future date, then we also have to put the promise of the new covenant at a future date. Then His mercy to unrighteousness and His forgiveness of sins would have to be some other time because that's the covenant. It's all the same.

I will not eat with you until that kingdom day, but my new covenant is when it begins—your sins and your iniquities will I remember no more. So if we take that, we have to take the other two that the kingdom promises aren't right now.

So when we take communion and we hold that cup in our hand, or in the morning or any time when we have wonderful communion with God, Jesus Himself is supping with us. He's there. If you ever want to get close up in His presence at communion—look across the table so to speak—Jesus is there. He's there supping with you.

Remember, communion is a two-way street. Just one person doing all the talking isn't communion. So Jesus said, "I'm feeding you of My life, but you are feeding Me with your life because I feed on your worship, on your love." When He told the disciples, "I have meat to eat that you know not of," He wasn't eating something else, He was merely drawing from the adoration of a person whom He was leading to Himself. And when Martha said, "Lord, command that lazy sister of mine to get out here and help get your meal ready," Jesus said, "I'm eating right now. This is the best meal Mary's giving me. I'm feeding, I'm having communion—there's oneness of spirit." So what the Lord is telling us is that when I finish my sacrifice and the old covenant is done away, and I bring in the new, then we are going to have another time of communion together.

EPILOGUE

I F YOU READ the introduction to this book, you will remember that God sent a message to my uncle and told him to write down seven truths that were God's priorities. This book contains the vital teachings on the very first priority—the precious blood of Jesus.

After reading the last few chapters of this book, you may already have an idea what the angel told Roland Buck was God's second priority. Do you want to take a guess? The second priority God wanted Roland to write down was that God wants fellowship and communion with His people. The blood of Jesus frees us from sin, hallelujah, but God's intention from the beginning of time was to create people in His image, who had a free will to love Him or reject Him. The blood of Jesus gives us access to an intimate relationship with God.

God longs for His highest of creation (you and me). He yearns to walk with us and talk with us and be our friend. Of course, a friendship isn't a friendship and a marriage isn't really a marriage unless both people have a free will and equal right to reject or accept, to hurt or nurture the other person in that relationship. God wants a special, accepting, nurturing, and fulfilling relationship with you and me, and so I'll be honored to share this teaching and perhaps a few more in the next book. I hope you'll join us.

If God spoke to your heart while reading this book, I'd like to hear from you. Please send me a note by email to faithfulsteward7@aol.com.

IF YOU'RE A FAN OF THIS BOOK, PLEASE TELL OTHERS...

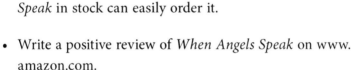

- Write about *When Angels Speak* on your blog, Twitter, Myspace, or Facebook page.

- Suggest *When Angels Speak* to friends.

- When you're in a bookstore, ask them if they carry the book. The book is available through all major distributors so any bookstore that does not have *When Angels Speak* in stock can easily order it.

- Write a positive review of *When Angels Speak* on www.amazon.com.

- Send me suggestions on websites, conferences, and events you know of where this book could be offered.

- Purchase additional copies to give away as gifts.

CONNECT WITH ME...

If you'd like to learn more about *When Angels Speak* please visit my website at www.rolandbuck.com. I can also be contacted on my Facebook page at http://www.facebook.com/timothy.holt2, phone at 626.377.0163, or contact my publisher directly:

HigherLife Development Services, Inc.
400 Fontana Circle
Building 1—Suite 105
Oviedo, Florida 32765
Phone: (407) 563-4806
Email: info@ahigherlife.com

CPSIA information can be obtained at www.ICGtesting.com
Printed in the USA
LVOW090708210612

287054LV00003B/1/P